THE GENIUS DECISION

Published by Spring Publications, Inc.
www.springpublications.com

Second, revised and expanded edition 2015

ISBN: 978-0-88214-592-1

Library of Congress Control Number: 2015931206

The paper used in this publication meets the minimum requirements of the American National Standard for Information Sciences – Permanence of Paper for Printed Library Materials, ANSI Z39.48–1992

KLAUS
OTTMANN

THE GENIUS DECISION

The Extraordinary and the Postmodern Condition

SECOND, REVISED AND EXPANDED EDITION

SPRING PUBLICATIONS
THOMPSON, CONN.

For Leslie

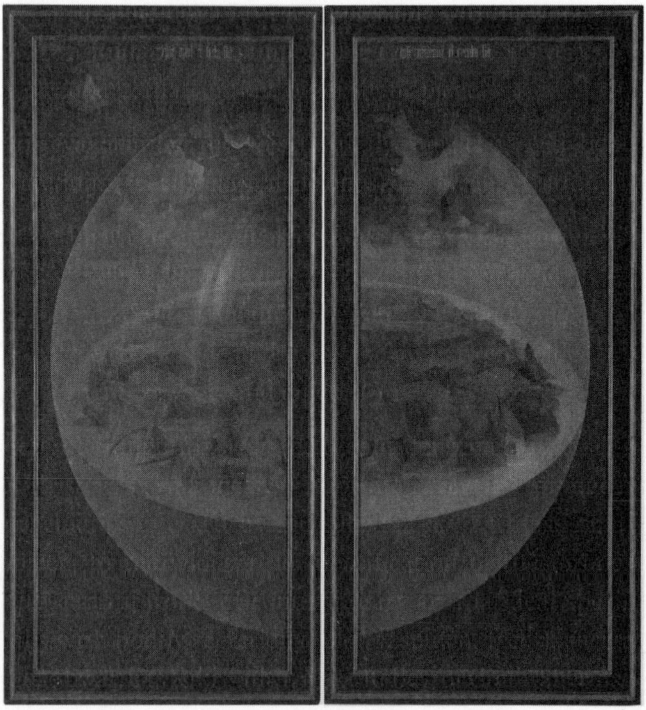

Hieronymus Bosch, *The Garden of Earthly Delights*
(outer panels)
c. 1500–1505
Grisaille on panel
Museo Nacional del Prado, Madrid

CONTENTS

PART I: ARGUMENT

PART II: EXPOSITION

PART III: CONCLUSION

PART I: ARGUMENT

What *is* the decision at all? Not *choice.* Choosing always involves only what is pregiven and can be taken or rejected.

De-cision [*Ent-scheidung*] here means grounding and creating...

But is that not here and everywhere a presumption and impossibility at the same time? ... Yes and no...

Who decides? Everyone, even in not-deciding and not wanting to hear of it, in dodging the preparation.

What stands for decision? We ourselves? Who are we?...

Thus decision is meant in an exceptional sense, thus also the talk of outermost decision that is simultaneously innermost...

But why and how to prepare for this decision?

–Martin Heidegger

1 / *The Question of Genius*

HOW DOES ONE ACCOUNT for those extraordinary and exceptional works of art and literature that set one artist apart from the others; works that most artists, however skilled, would never be able to produce; that exert a profound influence on others? This *disruption* of the ordinary, introduced into history by artists and writers such as Marcel Duchamp, Mark Rothko, Franz Kafka, or James Joyce cannot be explained solely in geographical, cultural, or formal terms. In fact, the extraordinary cannot be explained at all. The event of the extraordinary in art remains inexplicable–a mystery that is traditionally described by the notion of genius. Because it was widely abused in the past,[1] it has been applied in present art or literary theory by relatively few,[2] and then always at their peril. One of those few,

---

1 See W.R. Bett, *The Infirmities of Genius* (London: Christopher Johnson, 1952), an anthology of mostly nineteenth-century essays on genius, includes texts by, among others, Thomas Carlyle, Edgar Allan Poe, Charles Baudelaire, and Lord Byron. As an example of the numerous "scientific" nineteenth-century literature on genius, see C. Lombroso, *The Man of Genius* (London: Walter Scott, 1891), which contains chapters on the meteorological and climatic influences on genius.

2 Notable newer writings on genius include: J. Gleick, *Genius: The Life and Science of Richard Feynman* (New York: Pantheon 1992); J. Kristeva, *Hannah Arendt*, trans. R. Guberman (New York: Columbia University Press, 2001); P. Kivy, *The Possessor and the Possessed: Händel, Mozart, Beethoven, and the Idea of Musical Genius* (New Haven: Yale University Press, 2001); S. Schama, *Rembrandt's Eyes* (London: Allen Lane/Penguin Press, 1999); H. Bloom, *Genius: A Mosaic of One Hundred Exemplary*

Julia Kristeva, writes in her trilogy on "female genius" that genius indicates "a mystery that transforms the creator into somebody incomparable."[3]

In 1865, Walter Bagehot, the editor of *The Economist*, summarized his argument in defense of the constitutional British monarchy with the words, "We must not let daylight in upon magic." Clearly, to let daylight in upon the mystery of genius is a treacherous undertaking complicated by age-old myths.[4] Long before Charles Darwin's cousin Francis Galton published *Hereditary Genius* in 1869, a study that defined "genius" as "an ability that was exceptionally high and at the same time inborn,"[5] the notion of genius, of extraordinary and exceptional artistic talent, had been explained by Plato as divine inspiration, by Longinus as possession of godlike powers, and by Immanuel Kant as *Naturgabe* (gift of nature), an "innate disposition (*ingenium*) through which nature gives rule to art."[6] Sigmund Freud, when confronted with

Creative Minds (New York: Warner Books, 2002); M. Gladwell, *Blink: The Power of Thinking Without Thinking* (New York: Little, Brown and Co., 2005); M. Gladwell, *Outliers: The Story of Success* (New York: Little, Brown and Company, 2008); D.M. McMahon, *Divine Fury: A History of Genius* (New York: Basic Books, 2013); and C.F.B. Miller. "The Formation of Genius," in *Becoming Picasso: Paris 1901*, ed. B. Wright, exh. cat. Courtauld Institute of Art (London, 2013).

3 Kristeva, *Hannah Arendt*, 8.

4 As Jacques Derrida's comments, "This noun, 'genius,' as we are all too conscious, makes us squirm, and so it has for a long time." (J. Derrida, *Geneses, Genealogies, Genres, and Genius: The Secrets of the Archive*, trans. Beverley Bie Brahic [New York: Columbia University Press, 2006], 3)

5 F. Galton, *Hereditary Genius: An Inquiry into Its Laws and Consequences* (Honolulu: University Press of the Pacific, 2001), 26 ("Prefatory Chapter to the Edition of 1892").

6 I. Kant, *Kritik der Urteilskraft*, in *Werkausgabe* [WA], ed. W. Weischedel (Frankfurt am Main: Suhrkamp, 1977), vol. 10: A 179 (my translation and hereafter).

Leonardo da Vinci's "unanalyzable artistic gift," admitted to the utter failure of psychoanalysis in explaining artistic creation:

> We should be most glad to give an account of the way in which artistic activity derives from the primal instincts of the mind if it were not just here that our capacities fail us.[7]

7 S. Freud, *Leonardo da Vinci: A Memory of His Childhood*, trans. E. Jones (Abingdon: Routledge, 2014), 91.

2 / *Physical and Accidental Genius*

NEWER ATTEMPTS at explaining genius have focused mostly on "physical genius," the ability to recognize technological possibilities that no one had seen before: a high level of skill characterized by an abandoning of traditional methods and, often intuitively, the breaking of new ground or a shift in paradigm. In a *New Yorker* article, Malcolm Gladwell investigates the physical genius of athletes and neurosurgeons:

> What sets physical genius apart from other people... is not merely being able to do something but knowing what to do – their capacity to pick up on subtle patterns that others generally miss. This is what we mean when we say that great athletes have a "feel" for the game, or that they "see" the court or the field or the ice in a special way... Neurosurgeons say that when the very best surgeons operate they always know where they are going... [They possess] an ability to calculate the diversions and to factor in the interruptions when faced with a confusing mass of blood and tissue.[1]

Gladwell quotes sociologist Charles Bosk who conducted interviews with young doctors during their neurosurgical training in order to find out what separated the successful

1 M. Gladwell, "The Physical Genius," *The New Yorker* (August 2, 1999), 59.

from the unsuccessful. Bosk concluded that "far more than technical skills or intelligence, what was necessary for success was... a practical-minded obsession with the possibility and the consequences of failure."[2] Those doctors who admitted their mistakes turned out to be the most successful surgeons, while those who never made mistakes, usually didn't finish the program. Its anecdotal character notwithstanding, Bosk's research points to the significance of "failure" in explaining special or extraordinary skills.

Physical genius needs to be distinguished from what I would call, for lack of a better term, "accidental genius": extraordinary achievements that result from chance influences, unintended consequences, or even genetic disorders such as autism,[3] rather than intentional decisions or extraordinary physical abilities. In another *New Yorker* article, the artist David Hockney discusses his research into the possible use of optical devices by sixteenth-century painters, which he believes better explains the spectacular development of portrait painting in that brief period of time. According to Hockney's theory, the achievements of painters such as Caravaggio and Raphael may have been less indebted to their physical skills than to the accidental discovery of a pre-photographic device.[4]

One might consider the career of Walker Evans as an example of accidental genius. Regarded by many the pre-

---

2 Ibid., 60.

3 Cf. S. Silberman, "The Key to Genius," *Wired* 11.12 (December 2003), 226–29; 255–58; A. Snyder, "Savant for a Day," *The New York Times Magazine* (June 22, 2003).

4 L. Weschler, "The Looking Glass: How did the Old Masters draw so well? The modern master David Hockney has a theory that challenges five hundred years of art history," *The New Yorker* (January 31, 2000), 65–75. See also D. Hockney, *Secret Knowledge: Rediscovering the Lost Techniques of the Old Masters* (New York: Viking Press, 2001).

eminent American photographer of the twentieth century, a recent biography suggests that much of his "genius" may have been instigated by those he befriended or whose presence he sought out, including the writer James Joyce, the poet Hart Crane, and the painter Diego Rivera. Still others guided Evans's "unintentional" creative decisions, including his friend Paul Grot who introduced him to the miniature Leica camera; Hart Crane who asked Evans to contribute three photographs of the Brooklyn Bridge for the publication of his major poem, *The Bridge*; and particularly Lincoln Kirstein, the editor and artist-impresario with close ties to the newly founded Museum of Modern Art in New York. Throughout his life, Evans seemed to have been aware but never quite part of the major modernist movements – more a bystander than a participant. His 1937 retrospective at MoMA, the first ever one-person show of a photographer in that museum, gave him instant recognition, thanks to an unprecedented publicity campaign conducted by Kirstein's partner, Thomas Dabny Mabry, who worked at the museum: "[Mabry] mapped out an aggressive publicity strategy, beginning with a discreet 'whispering campaign,' to carry the news of the museum's one-man photography show by word of mouth. Then on to the literary journals, the Sunday papers (offering one exclusive photograph to the rotogravure sections of *The New York Times* and the *Herald Tribune*)... He made it clear that the exhibition was equal in importance to all other artists' retrospectives the museum had undertaken."[5]

An often-cited example of accidental genius is that of the French commercial photographer Eugène Atget who in 1898 began to document Paris, selling his images mostly

5 B. Rathbone, *Walker Evans: A Biography* (Boston: Houghton Mifflin Co., 1995), 157.

to artists, architects, and publishing houses. His straightforward images were praised in the 1920s by the French Surrealists for their modernity and included in a number of their publications. However, his photographs were not widely considered to have artistic value until the American photographer Berenice Abbott, who had met Atget while working as Man Ray's assistant in Paris, acquired the bulk of his estate at his death in 1927 and published a monograph on the photographer in 1930.[6] Her archive of Atget's images is now owned by the Museum of Modern Art in New York. Abbott later described Atget's photographs as "the shock of realism unadorned."[7]

The extraordinary paintings of Mark Rothko may serve as examples of creative achievements that cannot be explained by physical or accidental genius alone. Rothko, like Evans, is one of the most celebrated American artists of the past century. He was extremely well-read; yet, few books influenced him as much as Nietzsche's *The Birth of Tragedy*, which led him to eventually abandon figuration in favor of abstraction. Rothko's passion for music and fascination with the theater met with Nietzsche's belief in the restorative power of Richard Wagner's musical drama. In music, a sound evokes emotion at the very moment of its execution. Afterwards, only absence remains. Nietzsche regarded this as the core of tragedy.

Rothko used color primarily as an emotional vehicle. Paradoxically, he increased the emotional content of his paintings by reducing shapes and colors, choosing abstraction as a means of expressing the human condition in all its

6 *Atget: Photographe de Paris* (New York: E. Weyhe, 1930).

7 Quoted in I. Walker, *City Gorged With Dreams: Surrealism and Documentary Photography in Interwar Paris* (Manchester: Manchester University Press, 2002), 96.

complexities. Having painted in a figurative style for more than half of his life, Rothko's road to abstraction was filled with many obstacles (he suffered from constant existential doubt and anguish, and later in life, from a serious physical illness,[8] which ultimately drove him to suicide). He was obsessed with the idea that abstract painting could better express religious meaning and the full weight of the human condition than any other art form. Rothko's art and life were at once simple and complex. When asked, during his retrospective exhibition at the Museum of Modern Art in New York in 1961, how long it took him to paint one particular canvas that appeared to consist of a few formless blotches of color, Rothko responded, "I'm 57 years old and it took me all my life to do it."[9]

Rothko's monumental abstractions of ethereal fields of colors are unparalleled in Western art. He created his own rules: combining red and yellow didn't necessarily make orange. His paintings – their colors, emotions, sense of mystery, and meaning – cannot be adequately described in words: each is larger than the sum of its parts. Rothko regarded his canvases primarily as ethical statements. Guided by Nietzsche, he saw himself fundamentally as a *moral* artist, wishing to convey hope and faith in the good of human existence but also reflecting universal human conflicts:

> ... there is no yearning in these paintings for Paradise, or divination. On the contrary they

8 The last two years of Rothko's life were marked by the diagnosis of a dissecting aneurysm of the aorta, which put his life in a "downward spiral, battling alcohol and drug abuse, along with depression." (A. Cohen-Solal, *Mark Rothko: Toward the Light in the Chapel* [New Haven and London: Yale University Press, 2015], 196)

9 J.E.B. Breslin, *Mark Rothko: A Biography* (Chicago: The University of Chicago Press, 1993), 326.

> are deeply involved in the possibility of ordinary humanity.[10]

Rothko's art, as much about decision-making as about technical skill, is about "failing better," to use Beckett's words,[11] rather than succeeding. He illustrates what Rosalind Krauss calls, with respect to Picasso's "failure,"[12] "the splendor and misery... of the modern artist."[13]

Avital Ronell cites an exchange between Friedrich von Schiller and his friend Christian Gottfried Körner on the subject of Goethe's "genius":

> [Körner:] I cannot entirely subscribe to the comparison you made between yourself and Goethe... I greatly doubt that Goethe has more

10 *Writings on Art: Mark Rothko*, ed. M. López-Remiro (New Haven: Yale University Press, 2006), 143.

11 "Ever tried. Ever failed. No Matter. Try again. Fail again. Fail better." (S. Beckett, *Worstward Ho* [London: John Calder, 1983], 7)

12 See J. Berger, *The Success and Failure of Picasso* (New York: Vintage Books, 1989). More recently, Charles F. B. Miller has argued against Berger that "Picasso's production and reception have been closely and problematically intertwined with the history of genius and its critique," and that Berger's verdict of Picasso's "nineteenth-century type of genius... [had] little to do with his work." Miller concludes that "the conventions of genius were concomitant with the conventions of painting. We can redeem Picasso from one no more readily than the other... To think critically about genius must, in the first place, be to recognize it as an historical effect of signification." (C.F.B. Miller, "The Formation of Genius," [see chap. 1, n. 2] 85, 103) In his forthcoming book, *Radical Picasso: Surrealism and the Theory of the Avant-Garde* (Berkeley: University of California Press), Miller disputes the art-historical consensus that Picasso's production during two periods, 1926 and 1936–37, when the artist essentially gave up painting, were failures, arguing instead that Picasso "explored a number of different kinds of negativity, contradiction, and indeterminacy."

13 R.E. Krauss, *The Picasso Papers* (New York: Farrar, Straus and Giroux, 1998), 21.

> genius than you. He may have more technical skill [*Kunstfertigkeit*] in some fields, however.
>
> [Schiller:] This person, this Goethe, is just in my way; and he so often reminds me that fate has treated me harshly. How easily was his genius carried by fate, and how, until this very minute, I must still fight![14]

It appears from this exchange that Schiller regarded Goethe mostly as a physical and accidental genius. Ronell herself offers the following characterization of Goethe's "Apollonian spirit": "... incessantly denouncing that which is weary or sickly, dissociating himself from ... unnecessary suffering ... [someone who] has known but evaded the abyss."[15]

14 A. Ronell, *Dictations: On Haunted Writing* (Lincoln: University of Nebraska Press, 1993): 55–56.

15 Ibid., xxi.

3 / *The* Sensus Communis Aestheticus *and the Resolve of the Antinomy of Taste*

FROM KANT TO ADORNO, philosophers have struggled to reconcile the notion of exception with the Christian principle of equality. It still resonates in the avant-garde's original promise to pull the masses along. Paul's letter to the Corinthians proclaims Christian revelation to be inaccessible to the wisdom of nonbelievers: God chooses to reveal himself only to those of simple faith (Corinthians 1:23). It announces a complete reversal of the classical notion of elitism: "God chose what is foolish in the world to shame the wise" (Corinthians 1:26). It is this reversal and Christianity's promise of salvation through truth that Nietzsche later attempts to undo with his *Umwertung aller Werte* (revaluation of all values). The Paulinian promise of equality gains center stage during the Enlightenment and culminates in Hegel's *Phenomenology of Spirit*. In it, absolute knowledge is knowledge for *all*. As Jacob Taubes remarks, "the classical concept of philosophy implies the thesis: the path to truth is difficult and only few can tread it, but *always* tread it. With Hegel a new concept begins: the path to truth is difficult . . . but in the end *everyone* can participate."[1]

Within eighteenth- and nineteenth-century aesthetics a fundamental change took place that shifted attention from

---

1 "Elite oder Avantgarde? Jacob Taubes im Gespräch mit Wolfert v. Rahden und Norbert Kapferer," *Tumult 4/Schulen der Elite* (1982), 65 (my translation; italics added).

the beautiful to the sublime, changing an originally populist notion of the avant-garde into cultural elitism. Empowered by the Enlightenment, the sublime became the instrument of bourgeois art in its aspiration to be autonomous of the prevailing academic culture, which expressed the taste of the ruling aristocracy. It led to the replacement of the universally communicable experience of beauty shared by the common consciousness with a noncommunicable experience of the sublime, which could neither be taught nor shared but, like "genius," was bestowed upon the cultural elite.

The concepts of the beautiful and the sublime stand at the turning point from the avant-garde to the elite–common consciousness and genius–and find their most extensive philosophical treatment in Kant's *Critique of Judgment.* Kant distinguishes between a communal, pluralistic judgment of taste, the *sensus communis aestheticus* (which refers exclusively to the beautiful and is characterized by a universal communicability [*allgemeine Mitteilbarkeit*] without mediation of a concept [*ohne Vermittelung eines Begriffs*]), and a private, individualistic feeling of the sublime:

> By the name *sensus communis* is to be understood the idea of a *public sense,* i.e., a critical faculty, which in its reflective act takes account (*a priori*) of the mode of representation of everyone else, in order, *as it were,* to weigh its judgment with the collective reason of mankind... Taste is, therefore, the faculty of forming an a priori estimate of the communicability of the feelings...without the mediation of a concept.[2]

2 Kant, *Kritik der Urteilskraft, WA* 10: A 155 (see chap. 1, n. 6).

Every aesthetic discourse since Kant's *Critique of Judgment* has been based on the exclusion of the common or "barbaric" [*barbarisch*] taste that is affected by charm [*Reiz*] and emotion [*Rührung*]:

> Taste is always still barbaric where it needs the admixture of charms and emotions in order to be pleasing or even make these the measure of its approval... A judgment of taste that is not influenced by charm or emotion... is a *pure judgment of taste.*[3]

According to Kant, this pure judgment of taste must be a pluralistic, *a priori* aesthetic principle:

> If the import of the judgment of taste, where we appraise it as a judgment entitled to require the concurrence of every one, cannot be *egoistic*, but must necessarily, by its inner nature, be allowed a *pluralistic* validity... found upon some *a priori* principle.[4]

Despite Kant's efforts to exclude common taste from the *sensus communis*, the specter of the common consciousness still haunts the *Critique*: Kant presupposes it but never delivers an analysis of common sense [*Gemeinsinn*]:

> The judgment of taste, therefore, depends on our presupposing the existence of a common sense... But does such a common sense in fact exist as a constitutive principle of the possibility of experience, or is it formed for us as a regulative principle by a still higher principle of

3 Ibid., 10: A 38.
4 Ibid., 10: A 129.

> reason? Is taste, in other words, a natural and original faculty, or is it only the idea of one that is artificial and to be acquired by us, so that a judgment of taste, with its demand for universal assent, is but a requirement of reason for generating such a *consensus?*... These are questions, which as yet we have neither the wish nor the ability to investigate here [*das wollen und können wir hier noch nicht untersuchen*].[5]

Kant's *sensus communis* is essentially an imperative, an "ought" [*Sollen*], a definition to which Hegel forcibly objected. He considered Kant's imperative solution of the antinomy of taste–the exclusion of common consciousness [*gewöhnliche Bewußtsein*] from the "science of art" [*Wissenschaft der Kunst*] as an "ought"–a major deficiency of Kant's *Critique*. Hegel found his own resolve of Kant's antinomy in the "democratic" solution of the tragic conflict between two powers of equal justification, as demonstrated in Aeschylus's play *Oresteia*, in which the patriarchal law (represented by the matricide Orestes) stands in opposition to the matriarchal law (represented by the Erinyes, the female deities who are bound to avenge the murder of Clytaemnestra and thus constitute a threat to the patriarchal society). The resolution of the conflict is negotiated by Athena and accomplished by way of a cunning contract between the State and the Erinyes, which are cheated out of political power by enclosing them within the depoliticized sphere of worship. Thus the Erinyes, the "Furies," become the Eumenides, the "Kindly Ones." In the *Philosophy of Right*, Hegel uses the same *ruse* to separate the area of

5 Ibid., 10: A 67 (italics added).

production from the Family sphere, which in precapitalist society is opposed to the State. This separation creates an extrafamilial factory system and inserts a capitalist middle class (the Bourgeois Society) between Family and State. The Family concedes its economic significance and political power to Bourgeois Society, which replaces it as the area of production. The opposition of matriarchal and patriarchal law is thus transformed into an opposition of State and Bourgeois Society. It is no longer a true opposition, as the Family is now excluded and women are redefined under the new qualities of "love" and "piety."

In his *Lectures on Aesthetics,* Hegel responds to Kant's question (as to whether the *sensus communis* exists as a constitutive aesthetic experience or as a regulative principle of reason) with the elimination of art by proclaiming the precedence of idea over form, of criticism over art. Hence it is no longer necessary to presuppose a common sense, as Kant did:

> But just as art has its *before* [*Vor*] in nature and the finite spheres of life, so too it has an *after* [*Nach*], i.e., a circle, which in turn transcends art's way of apprehending and representing the Absolute... For us art counts no longer as the highest mode in which truth asserts itself [*Uns gilt die Kunst nicht mehr als die höchste Weise, in welcher die Wahrheit sich Existenz verschafft*]...
>
> For the Idea is alone the truthfully real [*Denn die Idee ist das allein wahrhaft Wirkliche*].[6]

6 G.W.F. Hegel, *Vorlesungen über die Ästhetik I* (Stuttgart: Reclam, 1977), 169, 178 (my translation).

More recently, Luc Ferry has revived Kant's *sensus communis* by giving it a Rousseauian reading as "direct communication" [*communication directe*]:

> Kant takes up here, in the aesthetic domain, the famous opposition Rousseau worked out in his *Letter to d'Alembert on Spectacles* between the theater, symbol of the monarchy, of the indirect communication which goes through the intermediary of the stage, and the festival, symbol of democracy, of the direct communication where the spectators' eyes are not directed toward an external object but rather provide the show, among themselves.[7]

Ferry reads Kant's *sensus communis* as a radical philosophy of difference, because it sustains, in itself, difference as such, "the articulation of difference with the idea of common sense."[8]

7 L. Ferry, *Homo Aestheticus: The Invention of Taste in the Democratic Age*, trans. R. de Loaiza (Chicago: The University of Chicago Press, 1993), 96.

8 Ibid., 97.

4 / *The Genius Decision and the Question of the Extraordinary*

THE GENIUS DECISION is not an attempt at explaining or predicting genius. Nor is its goal to construct *a* concept or *the* concept of genius. Rather, the following should be considered as a *horizon* of conceptual events that constitute an *philosophy of desire* in the sense of Gilles Deleuze and Félix Guattari[1] within the ethical-aesthetical writings of seven of Western philosophy's most influential thinkers: Spinoza, Schelling, Kierkegaard, Nietzsche, Peirce, Wittgenstein, and Heidegger. Deleuze and Guattari describe such a horizon as a "plane of immanence": "Philosophy is at once concept creation and instituting of the plane... The plane is clearly not a program, design, end, or means: it is a plane of immanence that constitutes the absolute ground of philosophy, its earth or deterritorialization, the foundation on which it creates its concepts."[2] As Heidegger says, "thinking is not a 'doctrine' and not a 'system,' but rather must become actual history and thus what is most hidden."[3]

---

1 See G. Deleuze and F. Guattari, *Anti-Oedipus: Capitalism and Schizophrenia I*, trans. R. Hurley, M. Seem, and H.R. Lane (New York: Viking, 1977), which Michel Foucault calls, in his preface, "the first book of ethics to be written in France in quite a long time."

2 G. Deleuze and F. Guattari, *What Is Philosophy?*, trans. H. Tomlinson and G. Burchell (New York: Columbia University Press, 1994), 41.

3 M. Heidegger, *Contributions to Philosophy (From Enowning)*, trans. P. Emad and K. Maly (Bloomington: Indiana University Press, 1999), 59.

Following Julia Kristeva's concept of the Abject[4] as the haunting memory of the Nonrepresentable and the sacrifice of *jouissance*[5] pressing for representation (which, according to Jacques Lacan, takes place during the Mirror Stage,[6] the transition from the Imaginary to the Symbolic), and Jean-François Lyotard's definition of the Postmodern as that which puts forth the Nonrepresentable in presentation itself,[7] I propose that the Genius Decision originates in the pressing of the Abject's desire for representation (a desire that can never be fulfilled because the Abject is

4 J. Kristeva, *Powers of Horror: An Essay on Abjection*, trans. L.S. Roudiez (New York: Columbia University Press, 1982), 1–31.

5 There is no adequate translation for the French *jouissance*. "Enjoyment" comes closest, as it implies a sense of entitlement (as in enjoyment of property); however, it lacks the sexual connotation retained in the French verb *jouir* ("to enjoy" and "to come"). See the translator's note in J. Lacan, *Écrits: A Selection*, trans. A. Sheridan (New York: W.W. Norton, 1977), x. Lacan appropriated the word from his teacher, Alexandre Kojève (see chap. 5, n. 33).

6 The Mirror Stage was first introduced by Lacan in his lecture "The Mirror Stage As Formative of the Function of the I as Revealed in Psychoanalytic Experience," delivered at the International Congress of Psychoanalysis in Zurich in 1949 and later included in his *Écrits*. It should be noted that Lacan's Mirror Stage has been largely ignored within the practice of child psychology. Few references exist in the literature to the mirror recognition of a toddler as part of the process of self-assertion, and those contain no mention of Lacan. Cf. D. Davies, *Child Development* (New York: The Guilford Press, 1999); M.L. Lewis and Jeanne Brooks-Gum, *Social Cognition and the Acquisition of the Self* (New York: Plenum, 1979). Lacan's description of the Mirror Stage nonetheless continues to play a role in philosophical and cultural theory where it is still considered a viable concept; see, for example, J. Butler, *Bodies That Matter: On the Discursive Limits of "Sex"* (London and New York: Routledge, 1993) and H.K. Bhabha, *The Location of Culture* (London and New York: Routledge, 1994).

7 J.-F. Lyotard, *The Postmodern Condition: A Report on Knowledge*, trans. G. Bennington and B. Massumi (Minneapolis: University of Minnesota Press, 1984).

formless and unrepresentable); in the artist's act of *reflective* decision to make visible the conflict between the pressing of the Abject to be represented and its inability to be represented. It is a decision that can only result in a representation of *failure*. Or, to paraphrase Foucault, the artist must assume the role of the dead man in the game of art.[8] The only "success" lies in evidencing this conflict – that there is a Nonrepresentable. It is a success that can only be achieved through failure. *The Genius Decision* thus focuses on recognizing the Extraordinary in art as an *active, finite event*, and describing it *after* it has occurred in order to better understand it. Comprehension of the Extraordinary within the postmodern condition must, by definition, remain fragmentary and incomplete, and must ultimately fail – but *fail better*. The Irish writer John Waters has described this act of failure immanent in artistic creation most elegantly:

> There is no understanding the unexpected. In approaching the Mystery, the true artist understands that the object of inquiry will recede at a speed exponentially related to the effectiveness of the approach. The more we learn about who we are, the longer we glimpse of what is to be known, the more we understand how futile is our attempt at understanding. Art accepts this

8 "Writing has become linked to sacrifice, even the sacrifice of life... As a result, the mark of the writer is reduced to nothing more than the singularity of his absence; he must assume the role of the dead man in the game of writing." (M. Foucault, "What Is an Author?," in *Aesthetics, Method, and Epistemology*, Essential Works of Foucault 1954–1984, vol. 2, ed. J.D. Faubion; trans. R. Hurley et al. [New York: The New Press, 1998], 206–7)

> but, in accepting it, resolves to continue a search
> that is ultimately impossible.[9]

The question put forth here is the question of Genius. What is at issue within the question of Genius is the Extra-ordinary. Thus the question of Genius requires the question of the Extraordinary to be formulated. We are always already involved in an understanding of the Extraordinary, which is grounded in an intuitive knowledge, a *sensus communis*, or "certitude." The word "certitude" implies a leap of faith in something that needs no objective proof or cannot be subjected to it. It is the assured possession of truth by the intellect and applies to immediate, intuitive truths. It is on the opposite end of ignorance, which is simple nescience or lack of knowledge. Certitude, as intuitive knowledge, differs from belief in that the latter can be held as certain, but it also differs from opinions, testimonies, or remembered facts. Knowledge is certainty founded upon shared (experienced or taught) insight; certitude is subjective and immediate intuitive knowledge that can neither be taught nor shared otherwise.

Following Kristeva and Lacan, this investigation unfolds in a series of discourses that track the Nonrepresentable or Abject as an index for its desire to be represented (the desire for the Other or *jouissance*) within the writings of seven (post)modern philosophers. To paraphrase Hegel, there is nothing in heaven and on earth, which does not contain in itself both Being and Abject.[10] The Abject as the

9 J. Waters, *The Pursuit of Glorious Failure* (The Arts Council of Ireland, 2007), http://www.artscouncil.ie/uploadedFiles/John_Waters_FINAL.pdf (accessed 12/19/2014).

10 "There is nothing in heaven and on earth which does not contain itself both Being and Nothingness [*daß es nirgend im Himmel und auf Erden etwas gebe, was nicht beides, Sein und Nichts, in sich enthielte*]."

Nonrepresentable is treated here strictly in connection with the sacrifice of *jouissance* and only insofar as the pressing of the Abject brings about a decision unto the Extraordinary as part of the Postmodern Condition.

A mourning for *jouissance* (the acquisition of freedom and autonomy of mankind in exchange for a sacrifice of *jouissance*) is detectable throughout much of Continental philosophy (even though there are notable exceptions),[11] usually motivated by a nostalgic, restorative desire to regain a state prior to the sacrifice of *jouissance* by trading difference for what Slavoj Žižek calls "the fragile Absolute":[12] the *objet petit a*, the state of desireless Nothingness. This sacrifice appears under many names: the biblical Fall from Paradise; the sacrifice of Abraham; the sacrilege of Prometheus; Heidegger's "thrownness" [*Geworfenheit*]. Its most startling presence, however, manifests itself in the opening sentence of Wittgenstein's *Tractatus Logico-Philosophicus*, which reads in German: "Die Welt ist alles, was der Fall ist." Usually translated into English as "The world is everything that is the case," (which omits the double meaning of the German *Fall* as "case" and "fall"), it links philosophy, the search for knowledge, to the *original sin.*[13]

(G.W.F. Hegel, *Wissenschaft der Logik I.* Werke in zwanzig Bänden [Frankfurt am Main: Suhrkamp Verlag, 1969], 5: 86 [my translation])

11 Nietzsche was the first philosopher to celebrate difference and continuously reaffirm the sacrifice of *jouissance.*

12 S. Žižek, *The Fragile Absolute: Or Why Is the Christian Legacy Worth Fighting For?* (London: Verso, 2000).

13 See J. Taubes, *Vom Kult zur Kultur: Bausteine zur einer Kritik der historischen Vernunft* (München: Wilhelm Fink Verlag, 1996): "A sentence that rings and is meant to ring at once positivist and theological." (176, my translation). Cf. also Heidegger's "The world as such is the 'what-of' of anxiety [*das Wovor der Angst*]." (M. Heidegger, *Being and Time*, trans. J. Macquarrie and E. Robinson [New York: Harper & Row, 1962], par. 40 [translation modified])

But first and foremost a question has already evolved: How do matters stand with the Extraordinary?

PART II: EXPOSITION

For us, there is only the trying. The rest is not our business.
–T.S. Eliot

Without failure, no ethics.
–Simone de Beauvoir

I myself, to be sure, have excited the expectations of others by certain uncommonly promising strides; and what should I now answer, when they ask how I have fulfilled them?

And why *ought* I fulfill *their* expectations? O how burdensome it is–it may be true, I am some sort of failed genius, but failed not in their sense but in my own. Knowledge, what is it?

And if thousands excel me therein, do they excel what is in my heart?
–Heinrich von Kleist

5 / *Kafka and the Pressing of the Abject*

Writing As Failure

ON 1 APRIL 1912, Franz Kafka notes in his diary: "For the first time in a week an almost complete failure in writing."[1] Then, on 23 September 1912, after having finished his first major story, he writes,

> This story, *The Judgment*, I wrote at one sitting during the night of the 22nd to the 23rd, from ten o'clock at night to six o'clock in the morning. I was hardly able to pull my legs out from under the desk, they had got so stiff from sitting. The fearful strain and joy, how the story developed before me, as if I were advancing over water... The conviction verified that with my novel-writing I am in the shameful lowlands of writing. Only in this way can writing be done [*Nur so kann geschrieben werden*], only with such coherence, with such a complete opening of the body and the soul.[2]

And another time he writes, "The story came out of me like a real birth, covered with filth and slime."[3] Kafka's writing is associated almost by definition with *failure*, with its own

1 F. Kafka, *Diaries 1910–1913*, ed. M. Brod, trans. M. Greenberg and H. Arendt (New York: Schocken Books, 1965), 276.

2 Ibid., 259.

3 Ibid., 278.

abolition, or, to borrow a term used by Deleuze and Guattari, "its deterritorialization."[4] Kafka wanted to succeed in literature; instead he succeeded *by failing it*—by constantly tearing down his own achievements. Kafka introduces the practice of writing as failure in his story *In The Penal Colony* with the metaphor of a writing-apparatus, which is designed to inscribe the judgment onto the skin of the condemned-to-death, but ultimately fails to do so.[5]

The "writing" of the apparatus demands from the "reader" the ultimate sacrifice: death. Like Kafka's apparatus, the "star-writing" used by the American artist James Lee Byars,[6]

4 G. Deleuze and F. Guattari, *Kafka: Toward a Minor Literature*, trans. D. Polan (Minneapolis: University of Minnesota Press, 1986), 6.

5 "Now I know all about it,' said the explorer as the officer came back to him. 'All except the most important thing,' he answered, seizing the explorer's arm and pointing upwards: 'In the Designer are all the cogwheels that control the movements of the Harrow, and this machinery is regulated according to the inscription demanded by the sentence. I am still using the guiding plans drawn by the former Commandant. Here they are.' He extracted some sheets from the leather wallet. 'But I'm sorry I can't let you handle them, they are my most precious possessions. Just take a seat and I'll hold them in front of you like this, then you'll be able to see everything quite well.' He spread out the first sheet of paper. The explorer would have liked to say something appreciative, but all he could see was a labyrinth of lines crossing and recrossing each other, which covered the paper so thickly that it was difficult to discern the blank spaces between them. 'Read it,' said the officer. 'I can't,' said the explorer. 'Yet it's clear enough,' said the officer. 'It's very ingenious,' said the explorer evasively, 'but I can't make it out.' 'Yes,' said the officer with a laugh, putting the paper away again, 'it's no calligraphy for schoolchildren. It needs to be studied closely. I'm quite sure that in the end you would understand it too. Of course the script can't be a simple one; it's not supposed to kill a man straight off... There have to be lots and lots of flourishes around the actual script.'" (F. Kafka, *The Complete Stories*, ed. N.N. Glatzer [New York: Schocken, 1983], 149)

6 See K. Ottmann, *Life, Love, and Death: The Work of James Lee Byars*, exh. cat. Schirn Kunsthalle, Frankfurt am Main (Ostfildern-Ruit: Hatje Cantz, 2004).

a highly ornamental script that for the uninitiated can be extremely difficult to read, engages those who undertake to decipher it in an act of "deathly" complicity. Byars is known for creating works that are extreme in their formal simplicity, yet exceedingly luxurious in the choice of materials: marble, gold, black or red silk, and glass. Living in Japan during his formative years, Byars developed his unique style by adopting the highly sensual and symbolic practices of Japanese *Noh* theater and wedding them with Western conceptual art and analytical philosophy. Byars's objects are a reflection of his lifelong pursuit of the transient nature of beauty and perfection, which operates on both a perceptual and conceptual level, affecting the viewer in a very physical experience of a concept that is abstract in nature. He saw death as symbolic of perfection – at once attainable and elusive. While his earlier works, done in the 1960s and 1970s and mostly made of silk or paper, sought to dematerialize his objects through actions and performances, his later works of the 1980s and 1990s rematerialize performance by turning the objects themselves into actors that raise philosophical questions. In his performances and installations, he forced the viewer to confront mortality, as in his 1976 performance *The Play of Death*, in which Byars and twelve physicians, all dressed in black, appeared on the balconies of thirteen rooms rented in a Cologne hotel facing onto a public square. Byars made the sound "th" (for *thanatos*, "death"), after which all retreated back into their rooms. As in Kafka's story, for Byars, simply being an artist is a metaphor for death and failure.

In their book on Kafka, Deleuze and Guattari speak of "minor literature,"[7] which is defined by three characteristics

7 Deleuze and Guattari, *Kafka*, 16.

that may lead to a better understanding of the Extraordinary as failure:

> 1. Minor literature is always constructed within a major language. It is "the impossibility of not writing."[8]
>
> 2. Minor literature is, by definition, political; the individual concerns of the writer are indispensable and magnified.[9]
>
> 3. It is a collective, active-passive event; the scarcity of talent allows the conception of a collective genius, a collective "machine of expression."[10]

Kafka's *certitude* ("Only *in this way* can writing be done") implies acceptance, a certain passivity—a *pressing from within.* It is an *active* passivity, an active-passive decision by the *abjected* artistic Self that is *beyond intentionality.* As the world becomes perceived as nonobjectifiable, it nevertheless presses itself to be represented; it is no longer a *simple* matter of choice.

The Theory of the Abject

JULIA KRISTEVA BELIEVES that the state that precedes Lacan's Mirror Stage (the formation of the Self and the differentiation into Subject and Object (the move from the Imaginary to the Symbolic, to language) lingers on as a subconscious memory even after the formation of the Self. She calls this haunting memory the Abject:

---

8 Ibid.

9 Or in Kafka's words: "It is a purification of conflict . . . a matter of life and death." (*Diaries*, 194)

10 Deleuze and Guattari, *Kafka*, 19.

> The abject is not an ob-ject facing me, which I name or imagine... The abject has only one quality of the object – that of being opposed to I.[11]

Because the Abject exists prior to the "I" – the differentiation of subject versus object, form versus content – it is the Nonrepresentable. As such the Abject calls or presses from *within*. (Not unlike Heidegger's call of conscience, which "does not come from someone else who is with me in the world" but "*from* me and yet *from beyond me and over me* [*der Ruf kommt aus mir und doch* über *mich*]."[12] For Kristeva, the Abject is, above all, ambiguity: "While releasing a hold, it does not radically cut off the subject from what threatens it."[13] It is in this calling of the Abject that the Nonrepresentable enters the realm of the artistic self. Perhaps this must always be part of the Genius Decision: *a leap from the ambiguity of the Abject toward the certainty of failure.*

Kristeva defines the Abject as the "radically excluded," a place "where meaning collapses."[14] Like *jouissance* (which Lacan situates outside the body [*hors corps*], the Abject "lies outside," from where it continues to "beseech":

> There looms, within abjection, one of those violent, dark revolts of being, directed against a threat that seems to emanate from an exorbitant outside or inside, ejected beyond the scope of the possible, the tolerable, the thinkable.

11 Kristeva, *Powers of Horror*, 1 (see chap. 4, n. 4).

12 Heidegger, *Being and Time*, par. 57 and 275 (see chap. 4, n. 14; translation modified).

13 Kristeva, *Powers of Horror*, 9.

14 Ibid., 2.

> It lies there, quite close, but it cannot be assimilated. It beseeches, worries, and fascinates desire, which, nevertheless, does not let itself be seduced. Apprehensive, desire turns aside; sickened, it rejects. A certainty protects it from the shameful – a certainty of which it is proud holds on to it.[15]

Kristeva's Abject is modeled after Lacan's second-order Real (R2), a residue of the original Real (R1), which precedes symbolic language and signification and is left out in the process of symbolization. Lacan's R2 (also referred to as the "Lacanian Cause") is something unaccountable – a logical exception or paradox. R1 does not "exist," as it precedes language; it "ex-ists." Language causes the split of the subject (in its most basic self-presence) into Ego and Subject (the barred or split subject: $) – into a collection of ideal (mirror) images, which are always false, and the alienated barred subject, which must sacrifice part of its being in the process of symbolization. Just as Lacan's "Purloined Letter"[16] does not forget the one who has forgotten it, the Abject does not forget the barred subject. The unconscious cannot forget, and neither can the Abject.

Rosalind Krauss compares Kristeva's notion of abjection to a "borderline" condition in the psychiatric sense: an "intermediary position – neither subject nor object."[17] Abjection is a condition of displacement, of deterritorialization:

> Instead of sounding himself as to his "being," [the one by whom the Abject exists] does so

15 Ibid., 1.

16 "La Séminaire sur 'La Lettre volée,'" in J. Lacan, *Écrits I* (Paris: Éditions du Seuil, 1966), 21–75.

17 Y.-A. Bois and R. E. Krauss, *Formless: A User's Guide* (New York: Zone Books, 1997), 237.

> concerning his place: "*Where* am I?" instead of "Who am I?"[18]

The Abject "dissituates;" it deterritorializes. As Barthes writes about being subjected to *jouissance*, "it is at present out of place" – a "nonsite."[19]

Here it is interesting to compare the idea of the Abject as a "Non-Site" with the use of the term by the land artist Robert Smithson for whom the definition of "Sites" versus "Non-Sites" became central to his earth projects of the 1970s (which he called "abstract geology").[20] Working primarily in geological sites, such as quarries, with heavy machinery that disrupted the earth's crust, Smithson deterritorialized art by claiming geological "sites" as physical and historical extensions of artistic activity beyond the traditional studio. Collecting pieces of slate and mica taken from these sites and displaying them in austere minimalist containers in museums or galleries as "non-sites," he introduced the realm of the Abject into sculpture:

> The bins or containers of my *Non-Sites* gather in the fragments that are experienced in the physical abyss of raw matter. The tools of technology become part of the Earth's geology as they sink back into their original state. Machines, like dinosaurs, must return to dust and rust. One might say a "de-architecturing" takes place before the artist sets his limits outside the studio or room.[21]

---

18 Kristeva, *Powers of Horror*, 8.

19 R. Barthes, *The Pleasure of the Text*, trans. R. Miller (New York: Hill and Wang, 1975), 63.

20 *The Writings of Robert Smithson*, ed. N. Holt (New York: New York University Press, 1979), 82.

21 Ibid., 85.

Abject, *Jouissance*, and the Mirror Stage

THE ABJECT IS AMBIGUOUS; it lies "in-between,"[22] "between Inside and Outside."[23] It straddles the Imaginary and the Symbolic. The exiled subject "strays": "[It] is on a journey, during the night, the end of which keeps receding."[24] It is outside of itself, in the realm of Lacanian *jouissance* (which is always in the Other: "Man's desire is the desire of the Other [*le désir de l'Autre*]."[25] Kristeva situates the Abject "at the limit of primal repression"[26] in the drama that unfolds in the Mirror Stage:

> As in *jouissance* where the object of desire, known as [Lacan's] *objet [petit] a*, bursts with the shattered mirror where the ego gives up its image in order to contemplate itself in the Other, there is nothing either objective or objectal to the abject. It is simply a frontier, a repulsive gift that the Other, having become alter ego, drops so that "I" does not disappear in it but finds, in that sublime alienation, a forfeited existence.[27]

Lacan's Mirror Stage describes the infantile transformation from the child's insufficiency (its lack of resources) to anticipation of itself as an adult that occurs between the ages of six and eighteen months, when it recognizes itself for the first time in the mirror:

22 Kristeva, *Powers of Horror*, 4.

23 Ibid., 7.

24 Ibid., 8.

25 "The subversion of the subject and the dialectic of desire in the Freudian unconscious," in Lacan, *Écrits: A Selection*, 312 (see chap. 4, n. 5).

26 Kristeva, *Powers of Horror*, 11.

27 Ibid., 9.

> The mirror stage is a drama whose internal thrust is precipitated from insufficiency to anticipation – and which manufactures for the subject, caught up in the lure of spatial identification, the succession of fantasies that extends from a fragmented body-image to a form of its totality that I shall call orthopedic – and, lastly, to the assumption of the armor of an alienating identity.[28]

Jouissance is the desire of the child for the desire of the Other (or in Lacanian language, of the "mOther"). *Jouissance* is the jubilant affair [*affairement jubilatoire*][29] that occurs when the child recognizes itself in the mirror. But as soon as it sees itself as Subject, it falls prey to the Other; the sacrifice of *jouissance* occurs. The mirror image is a false image, which is already the result of a "castration,"[30] the renunciation of *jouissance*. It no longer belongs to the child but has already been handed over to the mOther: "Castration has to do with the fact that, at a certain point, we are required to give up some *jouissance*... What happens to the *jouissance* that is sacrificed? Where does it go?... [I]t shifts to the Other; it is, in a sense, transferred to the Other's account."[31]

---

28 "The mirror stage as formative of the function of the I as revealed in psychoanalytic experience," in Lacan, *Écrits: A Selection*, 4.

29 Ibid., 1.

30 "What is castration? It is certainly not like the formulations Little Hans puts forward, that someone unscrews the little faucet, for it nevertheless remains in place. What is at stake is that he cannot take his *jouissance* inside himself." (J. Lacan, *Seminar XIV*, quoted in B. Fink, *The Lacanian Subject: Between Language and Jouissance* [Princeton, N.J.: Princeton University Press, 1995], 99)

31 Ibid.

The Paradoxes of *Jouissance*

I PROPOSE that just as, according to Lacan, there are two conceptions of the Real (the Real *before* and the Real *after* the letter), there are at least two distinct manifestations of *jouissance*: the one *before* and the one *after* signification (J1 and J2). The second-order *jouissance* (J2) resides in the Abject—the leftover byproduct of symbolization. This handed-over, sacrificed *jouissance* (J2) circulates outside the body (in the form of writing, painting, etc.):

> The sacrifice of *jouissance*—and the extent of the sacrifice should not be underestimated, for it leaves behind "a mere pittance of pleasure"—is necessitated by the Other's demand that we speak... [It] is tied to all of culture, all bodies of knowledge.[32]

Lacan constructed his concept of surplus-*jouissance* [the *object petit a*] on Aexandre Kojève's discussion of Hegel and Marx and on his own reading of Freud. It is part surplus [*Mehr-lust*], part profit of pleasure [*Lustgewinn*]. Kojève first introduced the term *jouissance* in his comments on Hegel's notion of enjoyment [*Genuß*] in the context of the master-slave dialectics described in the *Phenomenology of Spirit*:

> For the Master, on the other hand, the *immediate* relation [to the thing] comes into being through that mediation [i.e., through the work of the Slave who transforms the natural thing, the "raw material," with a view to its consumption (by the Master), as pure negation of the object, that is, as *Enjoyment* [*jouissance*]... What Desire did not achieve, the Master... does achieve.

32 Ibid., 100.

> The Master can finish off the thing completely and satisfy himself in Enjoyment.[33]

According to Kristeva, *jouissance* is only experienced by the subject *as* Abject.[34] It is the "impossible *jouissance*,"[35] a "repulsive gift"[36] of the Other, that the "*jouisseur* master"[37] presents to the subject/slave as his reward for repressing his desire and handing over his *jouissance* to him. (Here Lacan's *petit m* takes on another meaning: it becomes *maître* (master). The Abject is a form of *jouissance* that cannot be enjoyed, but "is, above all, ambiguity" and as such constitutes "perpetual danger":[38]

> Because, while releasing a hold, it does not radically cut off the subject from that which threatens it–on the contrary, abjection acknowledges it to be in perpetual danger.[39]

In fact, *jouissance* is the very condition that makes the Abject possible. It is only accessible through *jouissance*:

> The Other . . . jettisons the object into an abominable real, inaccessible except through *jouissance*. It follows that *jouissance* alone causes the Abject to exist as such. One does not know it, one does not desire it, one joys in it [*on en jouit*].[40]

---

33 A. Kojève, *Introduction to the Reading of Hegel: Lectures on the Phenomenology of Spirit*, trans. J.H. Nichols. Jr. (Ithaca, N.Y.: Cornell University Press, 1980), 17–18.

34 Kristeva, *Powers of Horror*, 9.

35 M. Borch-Jacobsen, *Lacan: The Absolute Master*, trans. D. Brick (Stanford: Stanford University Press, 1991), 93.

36 Kristeva, *Powers of Horror*, 9.

37 Borch-Jacobsen, *Lacan*, 255.

38 Kristeva, *Powers of Horror*, 9.

39 Ibid.

40 Ibid.

The original *jouissance* (J1), which precedes the Mirror Stage and the process of symbolization, is *absolute*. It does not yet know itself as Subject (Ego); thus it does not yet know the other *as* Other. It exceeds the possibilities of desire.[41] But as soon as *jouissance* is handed over to the Other, it is desired again as the desire of the Other, who accumulates it as capital, as *surplus-Jouissance*. But it can never become absolute again, because it is a "strange surplus" at the "end of history": "That 'Sunday,' during which the Man-God was supposed to rest and contemplate his work, falls irreversibly into *désouvrement* (Blanchot), into 'useless negativity' (Bataille), into pure insatiable 'desire' (Lacan)."[42] A surplus of satisfaction creates a surplus of dissatisfaction. Lacan puts it pointedly: after the Mirror Stage, *jouissance* can only be "reached on the inverted ladder of the Law of desire."[43] J2 is located in the "curved space" of Žižek's "fragile Absolute":

> The surplus-enjoyment, the *objet petit a*... exists (or rather, persists) in a kind of curved space—the nearer you get to it, the more it eludes your grasp (or the more you possess it, the greater the lack).[44]

Mikkel Borch-Jacobsen regards this as Kojève's essential lesson to his students Lacan, Bataille, and Blanchot: that desire is always the desire for the desire of the Other.[45]

The Abject is situated on the "other side of the border" (death, the ultimate border symbolized by the corpse): the

41 *Roland Barthes by Roland Barthes*, trans. R. Howard (New York: Hill and Wang, 1977), 112.

42 Borch-Jacobsen, *Lacan*, 7–8.

43 "The Subversion of the subject and the dialectic of desire in the Freudian unconscious," in *Lacan, Écrits: A Selection*, 324.

44 Žižek, *The Fragile Absolute*, 21–24 (see chap. 4, n. 12).

45 Borch-Jacobsen, *Lacan*, 91–92.

"utmost of abjection" that is "death infecting life."[46] To paraphrase Kierkegaard, abjection is an existential border *unto death*: "I am at the border of my condition as a living being.[47] It is the "ultimate region of being," at which, according to Bataille, "philosophy, like all communal human determinations, only arrives in spite of itself."[48]

One is always already in the presence of the Abject, just as "the mirror has always been there."[49] The Abject precedes *jouissance*, which can only exist as loss, absence; thus desire can only be *jouissance if* it is first "abjected." Abjection is not the end of *jouissance*—the end of history—but its *beginning*. It is its condition. Lacan writes about being in the presence of the absolute master, "The image of the master . . . becomes confused in [Man] with the image of death . . . [Man] is in his presence from the beginning, whether he has been taught this or not, insofar as he is subjected to this image."[50]

The Abject exists prior to the symbolization, in the original *jouissance*, but it is not yet experienced as "abjection." This suggests that there are really two Abjects: A1 and A2. While A1 does not yet know the difference between desirable and nondesirable *jouissance* (between filth and cleanliness, etc.), A2 exists in the *différance* (to use Derrida's expression). Thus the Abject exists (as A1) prior to the Mirror Stage (and prior to J2). Derrida derived his concept of *différance* from Husserl's term of "return inquiry [*Rückfrage*]," a questioning of an origin's tradition in order to reactivate it.

---

46 Kristeva, *Powers of Horror*, 4.

47 Ibid., 3.

48 G. Bataille, *Visions of Excess: Selected Writings, 1927–1939*, ed. and trans. A. Stoekl, with C.R. Lovitt and D. M. Leslie, Jr. (Minneapolis: University of Minnesota Press, 1985), 133.

49 C. Clement, *The Lives and Legends of Jacques Lacan*, trans. A. Goldhammer (New York: Columbia University Press, 1983), 84.

50 Borch-Jacobsen, *Lacan*, 93.

In his introduction to Husserl's *Origin of Geometry*, Derrida writes, "The Absolute is present only in being deferred-delayed [*différant*] without respite."[51] The word *differer* (to differ) conveys two meanings for Derrida: "On the one hand it indicates the difference as distinction, inequality, or discernability; on the other, it expresses the interposition of delay, the interval of a spacing and temporalizing... We provisionally give the name *différance* to this sameness which is not identical."[52] Thus the silent *a* in *différance*[53] can also be read as the A of the obscure and silent Abject that is reactivated by the Genius Decision as "différAnce." *Jouissance* causes the Abject to exist, but in order to do so, abjection has to *precede jouissance*. This is a consequence of the temporal paradox that Lacan regards as a main characteristic of the traumatic cause, which suspends the laws of causality. It is related to Freud's notion of deferred action of memory [*Nachträglichkeit*], as it is described in the case of the "Wolf-man": a traumatic event is not "activated" until a second event occurs.[54]

The temporal paradox inherent in the Abject is reminiscent of Spinoza's dictum that the mind *is* an idea, while we ordinarily think of the mind as *producing* ideas. According to Spinoza, affections such as desire are modes of thinking, which can only exist if the idea of desire already existed prior to desire; however, an idea can precede existence:

---

51 J. Derrida, *Husserl's Origin of Geometry: An Introduction*, trans. J.P. Leavey, Jr. (Lincoln: University of Nebraska Press, 1978), 153.

52 G. Ulmer, *Applied Grammatology: Post(e)-Pedagogy from Jacques Derrida to Joseph Beuys* (Baltimore and London: The Johns Hopkins University Press, 1985), 46.

53 "The *a* of différance, therefore, is not heard; it remains silent, secret, and discreet, like a tomb." (Ibid., 17)

54 "Aus der Geschichte einer infantilen Neurosis," in S. Freud, *Gesammelte Werke* (Frankfurt am Main: S. Fischer Verlag, 1978), vol. 12.

> Modes of thinking, such as love, desire, or any other of the passions, do not take place, unless there is in the same individual an idea of the thing loved, desired, etc.
>
> But the idea can exist without the presence of any other mode of thinking.[55]

Hence the human mind is an idea, as the idea precedes thought:

> The essence of man is constituted by certain modes of the attributes of God, namely by the modes of thinking, in all of which the idea is prior in nature, and, when the idea is given, the other modes (namely, those of which the idea is prior in nature) must be in the same individual. Therefore an idea is the first element constituting the human mind.[56]

For Spinoza the *idea* of the mind must precede the mind; in the same way, A1 must precede J2 for *jouissance* to bring about A2.

Rosalind Krauss compares Kristeva's conception of the Abject to Sartre's notion of *visqueux* (sliminess) – neither solid nor fluid but somewhere in between: "A slow drag against the fluidity of liquid . . . this flaccid ooze may have some of the qualities of a solid . . . but it does not have the resistance of solids."[57] The Abject infects life and art by

---

55 Spinoza, *Ethica*, Pars II, Axiomata II. (All references to Spinoza's works are to the third edition of B. de Spinoza, *Opera*, ed. J. Van Vloten and J. P. N. Land, 4 vols. [The Hague: Martinus Nijhoff, 1914]; my translation and hereafter)

56 Spinoza, *Ethica*, II, Propositio XI, Demonstratio.

57 Bois and Krauss, *Formless*, 238. See also my "The Solid and the Fluid: Bartlett, Laib, Kiefer," in K. Ottmann, *Thought Through My*

simultaneously negating the self and asserting it; in fact, Kristeva writes, the self can only exist in opposition to the Abject:

> If it be true that the abject simultaneously beseeches and pulverizes the subject, one can understand that it is experienced at the peak of its strength when that subject, weary of fruitless attempts to identify with something on the outside, finds the impossible within; when it finds that the impossible constitutes its very being, that it is one other than abject.[58]

Kristeva identifies the Abject with the "unclean," with bodily secretions (specifically female ones), decay, and death:

> Loathing an item of food, a piece of filth, waste, or dung. The spasms and vomiting that protect me. The repugnance, the retching that thrusts me to the side and turns me away from defilement, sewage, and muck.[59]

Here one might be advised to consider Krauss's criticism of Kristeva's symbolic system of the Abject as "producing a thematics of essences and substances."[60] Krauss rightly objects to the widespread identification of the formless with certain works of contemporary art that deal specifically with bodily secretions (blood, semen, feces), such as those by artists Kiki Smith, Mike Kelley, or Cindy Sherman. As an alternative to Kristeva's *feminine* interpretation of the Abject, Krauss reintroduces Bataille's structuralist concept

---

Eyes: Writings on Art, 1977–2005 (Putnam, Conn.: Spring Publications, 2006), 35–37.

58 Kristeva, *Powers of Horror*, 5.

59 Ibid., 2.

60 Bois and Kraus, *Formless*, 245.

of abjection that originates in a sociopolitical discourse on the nonrepresented *Lumpenproletariat*, which exists outside of the bourgeoisie and the proletariat, and which Bataille developed into what he called "theoretical heterology": a concept of abjection apart from "objects of disgust."[61] Bataille thinks about abjection *operationally*, as *process* rather than in essentialist terms. Following Bataille's notion of abjection as operative, I would argue for an Abject defined by *operational ambiguity*, retaining Kristeva's characterization of the Abject as ambiguous and intermediary, while introducing an element of *decision* into abjection.

According to Kristeva, the straying within the Abject saves the subject from the risk it cannot help but expose itself to: "[The exile] has a sense of danger . . . but he cannot help taking the risk at the very moment he sets himself apart. And the more he strays, the more he is saved"[62] – saved by *jouissance*: "For it is out of such straying on excluded ground that he draws his *jouissance*."[63] Kristeva at once acknowledges the perpetual danger inherent in the straying *and* regards *jouissance* as a kind of savior, echoing Heidegger's quotation of Hölderlin: "But where there is danger, there grows also the saving power [*Wo aber Gefahr ist, wächst das Rettende auch*]."[64] Heidegger describes this saving power as "fetching something home into its essence, in order to bring the essence for the first time into its genuine appearing."[65] Thus the subject is saved by that which constitutes its greatest danger: *jouissance* as Abject. But as Heidegger reminds us, it is

61 Ibid.

62 Kristeva, *Powers of Horror*, 8.

63 Ibid.

64 M. Heidegger, *The Question Concerning Technology and Other Essays*, trans. W. Lovitt (New York: Harper & Row, 1977), 28 (translation modified).

65 Ibid. (translation modified).

not a "saving" in the common sense of the word. Rather, the Abject conditions the (artistic) self for the ultimate sacrifice, which is the leap out of the ambiguity of the Abject unto certain failure. Thus the Abject is not an end in itself. The Abject lies not at the end of the Genius Decision; its ambiguity presses for a decision. To choose is to either remain straying in the Abject or leave the Abject behind for the certainty of failure.

Extending Jean-François Lyotard's definition of the Modern as that which "make[s] visible that there is something which can be conceived and which can neither be seen nor made visible" and the Postmodern as that which "in the modern, puts forward the unrepresentable in presentation itself... [and] denies itself the solace of good forms,"[66] I propose that the Modern is that which recognizes the Abject but is still caught in its ambiguity, while the Postmodern abandons the ambiguity of the Abject for the decision unto failure. And just as Lyotard recognizes that a work of art can only become modern if it is *first* postmodern,[67] the leap out of the Abject—the decision unto failure—*is always already in the Abject.* It is a nascent part of the Abject.

66 Lyotard, *The Postmodern Condition*, 81 (see chap. 4, n. 7).

67 Understanding postmodernism as a *condition* rather than a historically defined period of time, Lyotard writes, "Postmodernism thus understood is not modernism at its end but in the nascent state, and this state is constant." (Ibid., 79)

6 / *Spinoza's Ethics of Joy*

Spinoza's Theory of Knowledge

FOR SPINOZA, knowledge of God is knowledge of "God or Nature," whose essence is equally and alternatively expressed by the infinite attributes of thought and extension. It is the highest kind of knowledge:

> The highest good of the mind is the knowledge of God, and the mind's highest virtue is to know God [*Summum mentis bonum est Dei cognitio, et summma mentis virtus Deum cognoscere*].[1]

The lowest kind of knowledge is opinionated knowledge [*opinionem vel imaginationem*], followed by speculative knowledge. The "highest kind of knowledge" involves an intuitive grasp [*scientia intuitiva*] of how the essences of dependent things (or "modes") necessarily spring from divine nature, as explicated in Part V of Spinoza's *Ethics*: "The third kind of knowledge proceeds from an adequate idea of certain attributes of God to an adequate knowledge of the essence of the world [*ab adaequata idea quorundam Dei attributorum ad adaequatam cognitionem essentiaererum*]."[2]

Spinoza's conception of intuitive knowledge of the essences of things is innately linked with his notion of active ideas. In Part II of the *Ethics*, Spinoza introduces the notion of ideas as *active conceptions* rather than passive perceptions:

---

1 *Ethica*, Pars IV, Propositio XXVIII (see chap. 5, n. 55).

2 *Ethica*, Pars V, Propositio XXV, Demonstratio.

> By idea I mean the mental conception which is formed by the mind as a thinking thing... I say conception rather than perception because the word perception seems to imply that the mind is passive with respect to the object; whereas conception seems to express an activity of the mind [At *conceptus actionem mentis exprimere videtur*].[3]

Thus Spinoza's notion of ideas as mental activities is connected to his notion of free will:

> Suspension of judgment is, therefore, strictly speaking, a perception, and not free will.[4]

Spinoza's Discourse on *Jouissance*

IN PART III of the *Ethics*, Spinoza states that we are active if we are the adequate cause of something taking place ("adequate" meaning a cause "through which its effect can be clearly and distinctly perceived"[5]):

> I say that we act when anything takes place, either within us or externally to us, whereof we are the adequate cause... On the other hand, I say that we are passive as regards something when that something takes place within us, or follows from our nature externally, we being only the partial cause.[6]

States of greater perfection and are identified with Pleasure [*affectus Laetitiae*]; states approaching imperfection, with emotions of Pain [*affectus Tristitiae*]:

3 *Ethica*, Pars II, Definitiones III, Explicatio.
4 *Ethica*, Pars II, Propositio XLIX, Scholium.
5 *Ethica*, Pars III, Definitiones I.
6 *Ethica*, Pars III, Definitiones II.

> Thus we see that the mind can undergo many changes, and can pass sometimes to a state of greater perfection, sometimes to a state of lesser perfection. These passive states of transition explain to us the emotions of Pleasure and Pain. By pleasure therefore in the following I shall signify a passive state wherein the mind passes to a greater perfection. By pain I shall signify a passive state wherein the mind passes to a lesser perfection.[7]

Both are still passive states. Only in the third kind of knowledge [*tertium cognitionis*], the knowledge of God [*Deum cognoscere*],[8] can *active* joys be experienced. As Gilles Deleuze comments,

> Myself, things and God are the three ideas of the third kind. From them flow joy, a desire, and a love. Joys of the third kind are active joys: for they are explained by our own essences and are always "accompanied" by an adequate idea of this essence... The third knowledge thus has no other formal cause than our power of action and of understanding, the power of thinking, that is, of God himself, insofar as he is explicated through our own essence.[9]

Spinoza calls the active pleasure or joy that arises from the fact that "mind contemplates itself and its power of action"[10] "self-contentment"[11]–a coming into a state of

7 *Ethica*, Pars III, Propositio IX, Scholium.

8 *Ethica*, Pars V, Propositio XXVII, Demonstratio.

9 G. Deleuze, *Expressionism in Philosophy: Spinoza*, trans. M. Joughin (New York: Zone Books, 1997), 304.

10 *Ethica*, Pars III, Propositio LIII.

11 *Ethica*, Pars III, Propositio LI, Scholium.

repose in relation to one's desires. He identifies man's power of action and its accompanying pleasure with the mind's highest good, with eternity of mind and love of God: "Spinoza . . . says that self-contentment is the highest good we can hope for. Thus, it seems, self-contentment . . . and knowledge of God are one and the same."[12] In this state of highest possible mental self-contentment [*summa, quaæ dari potest, Mentis acquiescentia*][13] lies also man's highest pleasure [*summa Laetitia*][14]–his blessedness [*beatitudo*] or *jouissance*:

> Thus in life it is before all things useful to perfect the understanding or Reason, as far as we can, and in this alone man's highest happiness or blessedness [*felicitas seu beatitudo*] consists, indeed blessedness is nothing else but the contentment of spirit, which arises from the intuitive knowledge of God.[15]

For Deleuze, "the *Ethics* is necessarily an ethics of joy: only joy is worthwhile, joy remains, bringing us near to action, and to the bliss of action."[16] It contains "a second, subterranean *Ethics*," a second version located in the Scholia underneath the first.[17] Spinoza's discourse on *jouissance* is found on this *subterranean* level of the *Ethics*. The path through the hierarchy of knowledge led by Spinoza is a *reclaiming* of *jouissance*–a return to the state "*before* the

12 M. D. Wilson, "Spinoza's Theory of Knowledge," in *The Cambridge Companion to Spinoza*, ed. D. Garrett (Cambridge: Cambridge University Press, 1996), 128.

13 *Ethica*, Pars V, Propositio XXVII.

14 *Ethica*, Pars V, Propositio XXVII, Demonstratio.

15 *Ethica*, Pars IV, Appendix, Caput IV.

16 G. Deleuze, *Spinoza: Practical Philosophy*, trans. R. Hurley (San Francisco: City Lights Books, 1988), 28.

17 Ibid., 28–29.

letter" (before language). It is the ultimate gift of the third kind of knowledge [*beatitudo*]. This gift of *jouissance* must be actively asserted, since religious revelation, which is passively received via miracles or signs), would constitute only inadequate knowledge. *Jouissance* is claimed by *love*, a love that is "common to all men [*omnibus hominibus commune est*],"[18] in the act of the *amor Dei intellectualis*, the intellectual love of God, which is a *labor of love*:

> Love towards an eternal and infinite thing feeds the mind wholly with joy, without any sadness. This is greatly to be desired, and sought with *all our strength* [*totisque viribus quaerendum*].[19]

In the *amor Dei intellectualis*, *jouissance* is One:

> Our essence is part of God, and the idea of our essence, a part of the idea of God, only to the extent that God's essence explicates itself through ours. And it is in the third kind of knowledge that the system of expression takes on its final form. This final form of expression is the identity of speculative and practical affirmation, the oneness of Being and Joy, of Substance and Joy, of God and Joy.[20]

This enormous goal is accomplished by the simple act of man loving himself. Yet "the simplest thing for us is the most difficult," notes Wolfgang Schirmacher:

> The role of man is as simple as it is true... He has no other task than to love himself... Is that not

18 *Ethica*, Pars IV, Propositio XXXVI, Demonstratio.

19 Spinoza, *Tractatus de Intellectus Emendatione*, 5 (italics added).

20 Deleuze, *Expressionism in Philosophy*, 310.

> egoism, ethically of less value than the demand to love your neighbor? Such presumption is a hidden defense. Because he who cannot love himself cannot love at all.[21]

The Deferred Sacrifice

MAN'S QUEST FOR KNOWLEDGE, as the very last Scholium of the *Ethics* declares, it is never-ending:

> The wise man, insofar as he is regarded as such, is not easily stirred mentally; rather, being conscious of himself, God, and the world by a certain eternal necessity, he never ceases to be [*nunquam esse desinit*].[22]

Love is the eternal truth that motivates all ethical acts. "There is no purer and loftier morality than Spinoza's; the eternal truth is man's sole purpose for his actions," writes Hegel.[23]

Yet, in Spinoza's mind, there is no original sin and hence no fall from Paradise. In his first letter to the Dutch Calvinist theologician Willem van Blyenbergh, he writes on sin and evil:

> For my own part, I cannot admit that sin and evil have any positive existence, far less that anything can exist, or come to pass, contrary to the

21 W. Schirmacher, *Technik und Gelassenheit: Zeitkritik nach Heidegger* (Freiburg: Verlag Karl Alber, 1983), 40–41 (my translation). Cf. Peirce's divergent view that "self-love is no love" (see chap. 10, n. 23).

22 *Ethica*, Pars V, Propositio XLII, Scholium.

23 G.W.F. Hegel, *Lectures on the History of Philosophy*, trans. E.S. Haldane and F.H. Simson (Lincoln: University of Nebraska Press, 1995), 3: 275 (translation modified).

> will of God . . . The will of God is identical with His intellect, thus the former can no more be contravened than the latter . . . Thus the will or decision of Adam regarded in itself was neither evil nor, properly speaking, against the will of God . . . Thus the command given to Adam consisted solely in this: that God revealed to Adam that eating the fruit brought about death . . . To ask God why He had not bestowed on Adam a more perfect will, is just as absurd as to ask, why the circle has not been endowed with all the properties of a sphere.[24]

It is this abnegation of sin and evil (and thus the sacrifice of *jouissance*) that made Spinoza's philosophy so "scandalous" for Hegel:

> Spinoza's universal substance scandalizes the idea of the freedom of the subject; that I am subject, spirit, etc. – the determinate is, for Spinoza, only modification. This is the scandalousness [*das Empörende*] in Spinoza's system; it produces resentment against it because man is conscious of freedom, the spiritual . . . Both theology and common sense have insisted upon it . . . that freedom is real [and] evil exists.[25]

Hegel also objected to the mathematical method used by Spinoza, which, lacking true understanding, is unsuited for philosophy:

---

24 Spinoza, *Epistola* XIX.

25 Hegel, *Lectures on the History of Philosophy*, 3: 260 (translation modified).

> Mathematical knowledge and method are merely formal in character and consequently altogether unsuited for philosophy. Mathematical knowledge exhibits its proof on the existent object as such, not on the object as conceived; the notion is lacking throughout [*es fehlt ihm durchaus der Begriff*].[26]

Hegel argued that Spinoza's knowledge is learned but not understood, for it lacks the labor of the "unhappy" or "split consciousness [*zerrissene Bewußtsein*]."[27] Spinoza's "thoughts" are not "self-conscious thoughts or notions":

> The content signifies thought as pure abstract self-consciousness, but it is an unreasoning knowledge [*vernunftloses Wissen*], into which the individual does not enter: the content has not the signification of "I." Therefore, as in mathematics, a proof is certainly given, conviction must follow, yet the matter fails to be understood. There is a rigid necessity in the proof to which the moment of self-consciousness is lacking; the "I" disappears, gives itself up altogether, withers away, like Spinoza dying of consumption.[28]

---

26 Ibid., 183.

27 Cf. G.W.F. Hegel, *Phänomenologie des Geistes* (Leipzig: Felix Meiner, 1907): "This unhappy consciousness [*unglückliche Bewußtsein*], divided within itself, must, because this contradiction of its essential nature is a single consciousness, always have in the one consciousness also the other." (139 [207]; my translation)

28 Hegel, *Lectures on the History of Philosophy*, 3: 286 (translation modified).

Hegel considered this absence of the split self-consciousness in Spinoza's system its major defect: *the sacrifice does not take place.* For Spinoza, Adam's original "sin" (his eating from the tree of knowledge) is only the first step in man's path to *jouissance.* Thus his path to *jouissance* is guaranteed; he cannot fail.

7/ *Schelling's Fragile God*

> There is no other principle of explanation for the world than divine freedom.
> –F. W. J. Schelling

> God lets the oppositional will of the ground operate in order to foster what love unifies and subordinates to itself for the glorification of the Absolute.
> –Martin Heidegger

AT THE TIME Kant's *Critique of Pure Reason* first appeared in 1781, German academic philosophers were embroiled in the debate between Faith and Reason, and Kant's *Critique* was originally regarded as yet another contribution to the discussion of the latter. Not until the publication of Karl Leonhard Reinhold's *Letters on the Kantian Philosophy* in 1786–87 did the significance of Kant's *Critique* become widely noticed.

Kant explained our a priori knowledge of the phenomenal world and justified the beliefs in that which lies beyond all experience–God, freedom, and immortality–by distinguishing between a knowable phenomenal world and the things-in-themselves, which we cannot know. Understanding cannot give us a priori knowledge of the things-in-themselves, only of appearances. Reason seeks to go beyond what is sensate but stops short of the intuition of the Absolute: "All our knowledge starts with the senses, proceeds from there to understanding, and ends with reason beyond which no higher faculty is found for elaborating the matter of intuition and bringing it under the highest unity of thought."[1]

Despite Kant's claim of having finally settled the debate between Reason and Faith with his *Critique*, the discussions were far from over. Kant's *Critique* led, on the one hand, to the metaphysical idealism of Fichte, Schelling, and Hegel, who sought to complete the Kantian program, each on his own idealist path; and, on the other, to a "nonphilosophy" (*Nicht-philosophie*) or "unphilosophy" [*Unphilosophie*] that claimed that Kant's critical philosophy had made room for a separate Philosophy of Faith alongside the Philosophy of Reason, and was discussed most notably by Hammann, Jacobi, and Eschenmayer.

Schelling's path, on which he first trod alongside Fichte but by 1801 increasingly on his own, was that of a "speculative physics" or Philosophy of Nature that sought to solve the "riddle of the world" (Leibniz's question "Why is there something rather than nothing?"):[2] "How is the Absolute able to come out of itself and posit a world opposite itself?"[3] Schelling's path led from the Absolute to the finite natural world:

---

1 I. Kant, *Kritik der reinen Vernunft*, *WA* 3: A 298 (my translation).

2 "The Principles of Nature and Grace, Based on Reason" (1714), in *Leibniz: Selections*, ed. Philip P. Wiener (New York: Charles Scribner's Sons, 1951), 527. See also his earlier phrasing of the question in "On the Ultimate Origin of Things": "You will never find a complete reason why there is a world at all, and why this world and not some other... it is evident that the reason must be sought elsewhere" (ibid., 345–46); and Heidegger's rephrasing in his "Einleitung zu 'Was ist Metaphysik?'": "Why is there Being at all, and not rather Nothing? [*Warum ist überhaupt Seiendes und nicht vielmehr Nichts?*]" in *Wegmarken*, 381 (see chap. 12, n. 28).

3 F.W.J. Schelling, *Philosophische Briefe über Dogmatismus und Kriticismus*, in *Friedrich Wilhelm Joseph von Schellings Sämmliche Werke* [*SW*], ed.

> As long as we *presuppose* matter, that is, assume that it *precedes* our cognizance, it is not even possible to fully understand what we are talking about. Rather than groping blindly among incomprehensible concepts, instead let us ask what we understand and *can* understand originarily. *Originarily* we only understand *ourselves*, and because there are only *two* conclusions, one that makes matter the principle of spirit, and the other that makes spirit the principle of matter, for those of us seeking to understand *ourselves*, there remains only one assertion: not that spirit arises from matter but *that matter arises from spirit.*[4]

Schelling propagated an intellectual intuition that enables us to imagine the infinite or Absolute within ourselves independent of sensate perception and rational thought.

In 1799, the influential *Intelligenzblatt* of the *Erlanger Litteratur Zeitung* hailed Schelling as "one of our truly first-rate thinkers and a true universal genius" for having the "great, ingenious idea of extending transcendental idealism to a *system of the whole of knowledge*, that is, of establishing that system not only in *general* but in *deed.*" It designated Schelling alongside Kant as one of the most important philosophers of nature: "Whoever lays claim to the title of *Naturphilosoph* must study the writings of these two scholars."[5]

K.F.A. Schellling (Stuttgart and Augsburg: J.G. Cotta'scher Verlag 1856ff., vol. 1: 310 (my translation and hereafter).

4 Schelling, *Abhandlungen zur Erläuterung des Idealismus der Wissenschaftslehre*, *SW* 1: 373–74.

5 Quoted in I. Kant, *Opus Postumum*, trans. E. Förster and M. Rosen (Cambridge: Cambridge University Press, 1993), 275n89.

In 1804, Schelling published *Philosophy and Religion*, mainly in response to Carl August Eschenmayer's *Philosophy in Its Transition to Nonphilosophy*.[6] Eschenmayer, a philosopher as well as a physician, sought to ground the natural sciences, especially chemistry (which, still bearing the stain of alchemy, had been singled out by Kant as not yet having achieved the status of an apodictic science) in Kant's theory of dynamics by way of two originary forces – attraction and repulsion – that produce various gradations of matter or potencies. He was praised early on by Schelling for applying the Kantian principles of dynamics "in genuine philosophical spirit [*mit ächt-philosophischem Geiste*]" to empirical natural sciences.[7]

Schelling maintained a lasting and uncharacteristically warm and collegial friendship with Eschenmayer who provided Schelling's philosophical development with crucial impetus along the way. Each publication by Schelling was countered with a corresponding article or letter by Eschenmayer, who carefully dissected Schelling's theories and often pointed out inconsistencies in his arguments. The "sharp-witted" [*scharfsinninge*] Eschenmayer was Schelling's most diligent and constructive critic.

But Schelling's book also represented a new approach to the goal initially set in 1801 with his *Representation of My System of Philosophy*, the first system of philosophy he had conceived entirely on his own, independent of Fichte, after having seen "the light in philosophy," which led him to philosophize, as it were, out of the Absolute itself: "All philosophizing begins, and has always begun, with the idea

6 C.A Eschenmayer, *Die Philosophie in ihrem Uebergang zur Nichtphilosophie* (Erlangen: Walthersche Kunst- und Buchhandlung, 1803).

7 Schelling, *Ideen zu einer Philosophie der Natur*, SW 2: 313.

of the Absolute come alive."[8] In *Philosophy and Religion*, he tackled the problem of the manifestation of the finite world and human freedom by evoking Plato and Spinoza, yet by his own admission he did not reach his goal "with complete determinateness" until 1809 when he published his *Philosophical Investigations into the Essence of Human Freedom*.[9]

While Schelling's *System* of 1801 was only the first of numerous works to construct an objective idealism, the fundamentals of the *System* Schelling conceived during his *annus mirabilis* remained valid until his death. As Horst Fuhrmans writes, Fichte's work "challenged him to come into his own, to draw up *his* system, which, in all its transformations, he would never again abandon."[10] Schelling regarded his *Philosophical Investigations into the Essence of Human Freedom* as a synthesis of both his *System* and *Religion and Philosophy*; he would later write that it was in the latter work that he finally overcame the rigidity [*Starrheit*] of Fichte's philosophy.[11]

As Schelling explains in the preliminary remarks to *Religion and Philosophy*, a second work in the Platonic style

8 F.W.J. Schelling, *Philosophy and Religion* (1804), trans. K. Ottmann (Putnam, Conn.: Spring Publications, 2010), 16.

9 "The author has confined himself to investigations into the philosophy of nature ever since the first presentation of his system (in the *Journal of Speculative Physics*), the continuation of which was unfortunately interrupted by external circumstances until a new beginning was made in *Philosophy and Religion*—which, admittedly, remained unclear due to the fault of its presentation. Therefore, the present essay is the first in which the author puts forth his concept of the ideal part of philosophy with complete determinateness... Up to now the author has nowhere expressed himself regarding the main points, the freedom of will, good and evil, personality, etc. (except in *Philosophy and Religion*)." (Schelling, *Philosophische Untersuchungen über das Wesen der Freiheit*, SW 7: 333–37)

10 *F.W.J. Schelling: Briefe und Dokumente*, ed. H. Fuhrmans (Bonn: H. Bouvier, 1962), 1: 231.

11 Schelling, *Einleitung in die Philosophie der Mythologie*, SW 11: 465n.

of a philosophical conversation was to follow the publication of *Bruno or On the Divine and Natural Principle of Things*, which had appeared in 1802.[12] "External circumstances," not further elaborated on by Schelling, prohibited the completion of said work, and in light of Eschenmayer's publication of *Philosophy in Its Transition to Nonphilosophy* Schelling decided to use much of the same material for a new work. Because it is the only work prior to the *Philosophical Investigations* that discusses the issue of freedom of will, it is regarded as a precursor to Schelling's 1809 treatise on human freedom.

With his book, Eschenmayer sought to accomplish for nonphilosophy what Fichte and Schelling did for philosophy. His criticism of Schelling boiled down to the questions of how the Absolute in Schelling's system can come out of itself and become difference. In Eschenmayer's view, this question cannot be answered by philosophical reflection, only by a Philosophy of Faith: "That higher act, which encompasses all but that which to include into philosophical reflection would be a fruitless effort, is *faith*, and it alone resolves the entire field of speculation in the most perfect manner by limiting volition and cognizance, but is itself unlimited and will remain unlimited for eternity."[13]

Schelling responded to Eschenmayer's criticism in *Philosophy and Religion* by proposing a new theory, that of the falling-away [*Abfall*] of the finite world from the infinite by way of a qualitative leap: "There is no continuous transition from the Absolute to the actual; the origin of the phenom-

12 Schelling, *Bruno oder über das göttliche und natürliche Princip der Dinge: Ein Gespräch*, *SW* 4.

13 Eschenmayer, *Die Philosophie in ihrem Uebergang zur Nichtphilosophie*, par. 76.

enal world is conceivable only as a complete falling-away from absoluteness by means of a leap [*Sprung*]."[14]

But Eschenmayer remained unconvinced of Schelling's solution. He wrote to Schelling's friend Johann Jacob Wagner: "Schelling has saved himself just as little with his idea of a falling-away (in 'Philosophy and Religion' 1804) as with his other attempts."[15] Eschenmayer and Schelling continued to be divided on one major point, which Eschenmayer summed up to Wagner: "Here is the point where I part with Schelling. For him God is the Absolute, for me the Absolute is the after-image [*Nachbild*] of reason, and God is beyond it."[16]

For Schelling, as later for Heidegger,[17] philosophy is "ontotheology"; there is no need for a separate Philosophy of Faith[18] or nonphilosophy in order to discuss the concepts of God, freedom, and immortality: "Any philosopher would be weary of not gaining a much clearer cognition of those same subjects through knowledge and in knowledge than what emerges for Eschenmayer from faith and

---

14 Schelling, *Philosophy and Religion*, 26.

15 Letter from Eschenmayer to J.J. Wagner, November 26, 1804, in *Schelling: Briefe und Dokumente*, 1: 320n.

16 Letter from Eschenmayer to J.J. Wagner, April 5, 1805, in ibid.

17 "Philosophy's questioning is always and in itself both ontological and theological in the very broad sense. Philosophy is Ontotheology . . . Schelling's treatise is thus one of the most profound works of philosophy because it is in a unique sense ontological and theological at the same time." (M. Heidegger, *Schelling's Treatise, on the Essence of Human Freedom*, trans. J. Stambaugh [Athens: Ohio University Press, 1985], 51)

18 He had already written in 1801 to Fichte, in rather terse tone, that "you have been forced . . . to transfer [the Absolute] into the sphere of faith, of which, in my opinion, it can be no more a question in philosophy than it is in geometry." (Letter from Schelling to J.G. Fichte, October 3, 1801, in *Schelling: Briefe und Dokumente*, 2: 348–56)

premonition."[19] Schelling stayed true to Kant's spirit by rejecting the idea of a separate Philosophy of Faith. Kant argued for just such a unity of philosophy and religion in the preface to his 1794 edition of *Religion within the Boundaries of Mere Reason*: "Otherwise one would have two religions within each person, which is absurd, or one religion and one cult... both would have to be shaken up so that they become mixed together for a short period of time, after which they would separate again like oil and water, with the purely moral (the religion of reason) floating on top."[20]

Schelling's *Philosophy and Religion* was written during one of the most eventful periods of his life. In June of 1803 Schelling finally married his longtime lover, Karoline Schlegel, who had received permission from Carl August, Duke of Saxe-Weimar to divorce her second husband, August Wilhelm Schlegel. At the time, Schelling, who was educated at a prestigious Protestant school, the Tübinger Stift (along with his friends Hegel and Hölderlin), was teaching philosophy at the predominantly Catholic university of Würzburg that had attracted many followers of Jacobi and Jacob Friedrich Fried, another declared enemy of Schelling. Consequently, Schelling's philosophy became the target of incessant attacks. As Xavier Tilliette writes, "by settling in Würzburg, Schelling stirred up a hornet's nest."[21]

The sharp, polemic tone of *Philosophy and Religion*, especially manifest in Schelling's preliminary remarks, was not directed at his friend Eschenmayer but at "the horde

19 Schelling, *Philosophy and Religion*, 8–9.

20 I. Kant, *Die Religion innerhalb der Grenzen der bloßen Vernunft*, *WA* 8: B XXIII–XXIV (see chap. 1, n. 6).

21 X. Tilliette, *Schelling: Biographie*, trans. S. Schaper (Stuttgart: Klett-Cotta, 2004), 145 (my translation).

of rowdy opponents"[22] led by two influential high-school teachers from Munich, Kajetan Weiller and Jacob Salat, who, according to Tilliette, "dedicated their lives to pillorying Schelling."[23] Fuhrmans describes the attacks against Schelling in 1803 as a "furious drumfire": "In lowbrow reviews and endless polemic commentaries and publications, an assault was launched against the new 'obscurants' and 'mystics,' the 'hierophants of the new Eleusinian mystery cults' in order to defend against the advance or even victory of the Romantic mindset."[24]

Schelling's book on religion and philosophy itself, however, was largely ignored, as Schelling himself noted in obvious consternation in 1809. Its reputation may have become tarnished early on by Schelling's own admission of its faulty presentation. In a letter to Eschenmayer, written shortly after he had sent him a copy of his book, Schelling provided Eschenmayer with clarifications in regard to his definition of the Absolute: "It might be necessary to improve upon my in many instances faulty expressions as far as the main idea is concerned. Would the following exposition meet with your approval?"[25]

The cruel judgment delivered in 1887 by Heinrich Heine, who has been credited by Adorno with almost single-handedly dealing the death blow to the German Romantic soul,[26] did not help the stature of Schelling's book.

---

22 Schelling, *Philosophy and Religion*, 4.

23 Ibid., 144.

24 *Schelling: Briefe und Dokumente*, 1: 297.

25 Letter from Schelling to Eschenmayer, July 10, 1804, in *Schelling: Briefe und Dokumente*, 1: 321.

26 See T.W. Adorno, "Heine the Wound," in *Notes to Literature*, trans. S.W. Nicholsen (New York: Columbia University Press, 1991).

In *On the History of Religion and Philosophy in Germany*, Heine comments,

> Anno 1804 God finally appeared to Herr Schelling, full-fledged, in his book entitled: *Philosophy and Religion*... Here philosophy stops with Herr Schelling, and poetry, that is to say, folly begins.[27]

As Mason Richey writes so pointedly, Schelling "is the Don Quixote of nineteenth-century German philosophy; his philosophy is not beholden to a rule...when his work succeeds it does so spectacularly, and when it fails it does so spectacularly."[28] Schelling's works constitute a *minor philosophy* in the sense of Gilles Deleuze and Félix Guattari's definition of a "minor literature."[29] A minor literature does not come from a minor language; "it is rather that which minority constructs within a major language."[30] According to Deleuze and Guattari, a minor literature is "always connected to its *own abolition*."[31] It is a language "affected with a high coefficent of deterritorialization... [that] turns language into something impossible."[32]

Because of Schelling's determination to philosophize on the edge of the "originary abyss" [*anfängliche Ungrund*],[33]

---

27 H. Heine, *Zur Geschichte der Religion und Philosophie in Deutschland* (Halle: Otto Händel, 1887), 117–18 (my translation).

28 "Translator's Introduction," in F.W.J. Schelling, *Historical-Critical Introduction to the Philosophy of Mythology* (Albany: State University of New York Press, 2007), xvii.

29 G. Deleuze and F. Guattari, *Kafka: Toward a Minor Literature* (see chap. 5, n. 4).

30 Ibid., 16

31 Ibid., 6.

32 Ibid., 16.

33 Schelling, *Philosophische Untersuchungen über das Wesen der menschlichen Freiheit*, SW 7: 408.

i.e., in the face of the Absolute, his philosophy is associated–almost by default–with *failure*, with its own impossibility. In wanting to complete Kant's philosophy, Schelling ended up failing philosophy altogether in an endgame of theory by repeatedly tearing down his own achievements. Schelling attempted to philosophize out of the Absolute itself in spite of its impossibility.

In his study of Schelling, Slavoj Žižek describes the philosopher as "a kind of 'vanishing mediator' between the Idealism of the Absolute and post-Hegelian universe of finitude-temporality-contingency, that his thought–for a brief moment, as it were, in a flash–renders visible something that was invisible beforehand and withdrew into invisibility thereafter."[34]

This description echoes Jean-François Lyotard's definition of the postmodern.[35] By understanding postmodernism as a condition rather than as a historically defined period of time, as Lyotard does, Schelling could arguable be regarded as a postmodern philosopher because he put forward the Absolute as the unthinkable, as the *un*-grounds or *Ungrund* of that prior to which we cannot think [*das Unvordenkliche*],[36] in philosophy itself: "In presupposing a merely mediated knowledge of the Absolute (irrespective of how the mediation occurs), the Absolute in philosophy can only appear as something that is presumed in order that it can be philosophized about."[37]

---

34 S. Žižek, *The Indivisible Remainder: An Essay on Schelling and Related Matters* (London: Verso, 1996), 8.

35 See chap. 4, n. 7.

36 Cf. Schelling, *Philosophie der Offenbarung*, SW 14: 347: "The existing prior to which we cannot think [*das unvordenkliche Existirende*] precedes all concepts."

37 Schelling, *Philosophy and Religion*, 16.

Rather than executing a somersault that would land him safely on the ground, with one foot on reason and the other on faith, as advocated by Jacobi,[38] Schelling attempts a reverse *leap* into the Absolute within philosophy in order to initiate a "reverse formation [*Zurückbildung*] of difference into oneness"[39] that is a decisive leap in the face of certain failure.

As Žižek notes, the deterritorialized philosophy of Schelling speaks with three tongues: "the language of speculative idealism; the language of anthropomorphic-mystical theosophy; the post-idealist language of contingency and finitude. The paradox, of course, is that *it was his very 'regression' from pure philosophical idealism to pre-modern theosophical problematic which enables him to overtake modernity itself.*"[40]

Schelling's true folly was his attempt to construct an ontotheology at the event horizon of the Absolute or God. Leibniz's insight that the reason for our world must lie outside our world, in an extramundane entity–the Absolute or God–led Schelling to position his philosophy on the very boundary of the "originary abyss," which Wittgenstein later would call the "mystical," in an attempt to retrieve what is unthought and in some sense inherently unthinkable.

Schelling follows Spinoza's path of the *amor Dei intellectualis*–a love from which ensues a transcendental ethics that affects *care* for the world and the other through participation in God's essence. However, Schelling radically parts ways with Spinoza by placing the original sin–and thus failure–at the core of his Philosophy of Nature by redefining it in terms

38 F.H. Jacobi, *Über die Lehre des Spinoza in Briefen an den Herrn Moses Mendelssohn* (Breslau: Gottlieb Löwe, 1785).

39 Schelling, *Philosophy and Religion*, 33.

40 Žižek, *The Indivisible Remainder*, 8.

of a *Philosophy of History*. The theory of a falling-away forms the core of Schelling's argument: the original sin is not the Fall of Man but rather Creation itself, the fall of the finite world from the infinite or Absolute:[41]

> God is the *absolute* harmony of necessity and freedom, and this harmony cannot be revealed in individual destinies but only in history as a whole; consequently, only history as a whole is a revelation of God—and then only a progressively evolving revelation... History is an epic composed in the mind of God. It has two main parts: one depicting mankind's egress from its center to its farthest point of displacement; the other, its return. The former is, as it were, history's *Iliad*; the latter, its *Odyssey*. In the one, the direction is centrifugal; in the other, it becomes centripetal. In this way, the great purpose of the phenomenal world reveals itself in history.[42]

The final cause of history is the "reconciliation of the falling-away."[43]

Schelling's *Philosophy and Religion* was the first decisive step towards the formulation of a historicized philosophical religion that found its completion in his philosophies of mythology and revelation of 1856–58.

With his *Philosophy of Mythology*, which was the first philosophical investigation of mythology, Schelling emerges as a protostructuralist who already recognized that mythology is a type of speech, a mode of signification:

41 Schelling, *Philosophy and Religion*, 31.

42 Ibid., 44.

43 Ibid., 50.

> One could almost say: language is only faded mythology; what mythology still preserves in living and concrete difference is preserved in language only in abstract and formal differences.[44]

The methodology developed by Schelling in *Philosophy and Religion* and refined in his *Freiheitsschrift* represented the first step of a radical new approach in resolving the problem of the manifestation of the finite world and human freedom by asking not how Man becomes divine but how God becomes human through freedom – a freedom that as fragile as the God who is defined by it, who thus carries in Himself the possibility of nonbeing. As Sartre would later write, "it is through man that fragility comes into being."[45] It is through Schelling's ontotheology that fragility comes into the Absolute or God. It puts God on an equal footing with fallible man.

44 Schelling, *Einleitung in die Philosophie der Mythologie*, SW II: 52.
45 J.-P. Sartre, *L'Être et le néant* (Paris: Librairie Gallimard, 1950), 43.

8 / *Kierkegaard's Special Individual*

Kierkegaard's Subjective Minimalism

DESPITE THE FACT that Søren Kierkegaard's philosophy is driven (and ultimately confined) by religious motivations, his concept of irony and his "theory of the leap"[1] are distinctly postmodern.[2] As Schirmacher has pointed out, Kierkegaard's God "was already for him the god after the death of God, and his leap demanded a creative act without example."[3] Kierkegaard did not write a separate and clearly defined aesthetics like Hegel; yet arguably no philosopher, with the exception of Nietzsche, has written more on the creative act and understood better how aesthetics depends on an understanding of both the production and reception of works of art. In Kierkegaard's view, art is, above all, communication: "Artistic communication . . . would always demand reflection on the recipient, and an awareness of the form of the communication in relation to the recipient's

---

1 S. Kierkegaard, *Journals and Papers*, ed. and trans. H.V. and E.H. Hong (Bloomington: Indiana University Press, 1967), 3: 20.

2 Cf. C.O. Schrag, "The Kierkegaard-Effect in the Shaping of the Contours of Modernity," in *Kierkegaard in Post/Modernity*, ed. M.J. Matustík, and M. Westphal (Bloomington: Indiana University Press, 1995).

3 W. Schirmacher, "Indirekte Kommunikation und Ästhetische Ethik: Eine ironische Lektüre Kierkegaards," http://www.egs.edu/faculty/wolfgang-schirmacher/articles/indirekte-kommunikation-und-aesthetische-ethik/ (my translation; accessed 4 January 2015).

possible misunderstanding."[4] It is the potential for misunderstanding and ambivalence that caused Kierkegaard to choose abstract art over concretion, form over content, and ultimately abandon the indirect communication of irony for the direct communication of faith.

Kierkegaard's aesthetics is characterized by an inherent minimalism that is expressed in his glorification of "poverty" as it is bound to eternity:

> The more abstract and thus the more impoverished the idea is, the more abstract and thus the more impoverished the medium is, hence the greater is the probability that no repetition can be imagined, and the greater is the probability that when the idea has acquired its expression, it has acquired it once and for all.[5]

In fact, it is in poverty that the aesthetic and the religious coincide:

> Do you think it is always a kind of childishness on my part to look for the esthetic among the poor and the suffering; or have you demeaned yourself with that scandalous division that gives the esthetic to the aristocratic and powerful, the wealthy, the cultured, and gives, at most, the religious to the poor? Well, I do not happen to believe that the poor suffer by this division, and do you not perceive that the poor, if they truly

4 S. Kierkegaard, *Concluding Unscientific Postscript to Philosophical Fragments*, ed. and trans. H.V. and E.H. Hong (Princeton, N.J.: Princeton University Press, 1992), 1:70.

5 S. Kierkegaard, *Either-Or I*, ed. and trans. H.V. and E.H. Hong (Princeton, N.J.: Princeton University Press, 1988), 54.

> possess the religious, also have the esthetic, while the rich, insofar as they do not have the religious, do not have the esthetic either?[6]

It is this subjective (and minimalist) existentialism that becomes the primary target of Adorno's unforgiving Marxist critique of Kierkegaard's aesthetics:

> The abstract is defined as the temporally invariant, the concrete as the historically conditioned. Aesthetic ideas are for Kierkegaard *universalia post rem*, achieved through the exclusion of historically specific elements. His aesthetic thereby becomes ensnared in a nominalism that ultimately robs it of its object.[7]

Adorno did not live to see the emergence of minimal art, which began in the late 1950s with Frank Stella's and Ad Reinhardt's minimalist black paintings and Robert Ryman's white canvases, but he was familiar with Russian Suprematist Kasimir Malevich's "black and grey" paintings – "the most advanced arts," which "push this impoverishment to the brink of silence."[8]

Most sacred spaces are characterized by either a glorification of poverty – as in the asceticism of Protestant churches – or an exaltation of affluence – as manifested in the Byzantine mannerism of Greek-Orthodox churches. Both forms are bound to eternity, representing the opposite

---

6 S. Kierkegaard, *Either-Or II*, ed. and trans. H.V. and E.H. Hong (Princeton, N.J.: Princeton University Press, 1987), 127.

7 T.W. Adorno, *Kierkegaard: Construction of the Aesthetic*, ed. and trans. R. Hullot-Kentor (Minneapolis: University of Minnesota Press, 1989), 21–23.

8 Ibid., 40.

sides of this sacred aesthetics, and of a "negative apotheosis of color."[9]

Adorno acknowledges art's autonomy from reality,[10] but also warns of the danger of an empty formalism:

> The shadow of art's autarchic radicalism is its harmlessness: Absolute color compositions verge on wallpaper patterns . . . Among the dangers faced by new art, the worst is the absence of danger [*Unter den Gefahren neuer Kunst ist die Ärgste die des Gefahrlosen*].[11]

Form and Ideology

THE RUSSIAN FORMALISTS, Malevich among them, were the first to hint at the possibility of a formalism that does not eliminate content: an ideological formalism later adopted by Roland Barthes. Kierkegaard's existential formalism might be closer to this type of ideological formalism than to the "empty formalism" Adorno suspected.

The American critic Clement Greenberg, whose essay "Avant-Garde and Kitsch" has dominated American formalism since its publication in 1939, could be considered a modern descendant of the nineteenth-century German architect and art critic Gottfried Semper. Just as Semper defined art exclusively by the parameters of material and technique, so

9 T.W. Adorno, *Aesthetic Theory*, trans. R. Hullot-Kentor (Minneapolis: University of Minnesota Press, 1997), 135.

10 "Artworks detach themselves from the empirical world and bring forth another world, one opposed to the empirical world as if this other world too were an autonomous entity . . . By virtue of its rejection of the empirical world – a rejection that inheres in art's concept and thus is no mere escape, but a law immanent to it – art sanctions the primacy of reality." (Ibid., 1)

11 Ibid., 29.

Greenberg speaks of the "pure pre-occupation" of a modern avant-garde to dissolve content "so completely into form that the work of art or literature cannot be reduced in whole or in part to anything not itself" by means of inventing and arranging "spaces, surfaces, shapes, colors, etc., to the exclusion of whatever is not necessarily implicated in those factors."[12] Semper's mechanical-materialistic formalism was later challenged by the Austrian art historian Alois Riegl who proposed an artistic will or urge [*Kunstwollen*], which he believed to be an expression of the spiritual conditions of each period of time, thereby effectively introducing concept and ideology into art.

While Greenberg rejected formal meaning, a European version, originally proposed by Eisenstein and later adapted by Barthes, follows Riegl's model, recognizing form as ideology and engaging in an intimate investigation into the materiality of an object and its *functioning*. In a conversation with Guy Scarpetta, Barthes hints at a possible alternative to Greenberg's formalism:

> We should not be too quick to jettison the word "formalism"... attacks against formalism are always made in the name of content... The formalism I have in mind does not consist in "forgetting," "neglecting," "reducing" content... content is precisely what interests formalism, because its endless task is each time to push content back... It is not matter that is materialistic, but the refraction, the lifting of the safety catches; what is formalistic is not "form" but

12 "Avant-Garde and Kitsch," in C. Greenberg, *Art and Culture: Critical Essays* (Boston: Beacon Press, 1961), 6–7.

> the relative, dilatory time of contents, the precariousness of references.[13]

Instead of a mechanical-materialistic formalism, Barthes suggests a scrupulous examination of an object's materiality as *theoretical act.* It is this "structuralist activity" that defines the object. Materiality becomes structure, an "interested simulacrum," making "something appear which remained invisible, or if one prefers, unintelligible, in the natural object.[14] Adorno may have sensed this spiritual-political potential of art (in spite of himself) when he remarked: "The greatness of works of art lies solely in their power to let those things be heard which ideology conceals."[15]

Kierkegaard's existential minimalism became a continuing source of inspiration for artists. Minimal art, which became prominent in the late 1960s and early 1970s, was strongly influenced both by existentialism and structuralism. Unlike phenomenology, structuralism (which gained popularity in the United States in the sixties through the films of Alain Resnais, and the writings of Barthes and Susan Sontag) does not render the world as it finds it; it looks at the world's functionality, at the rules that describe its parts. Barthes defines structuralist activity as a "controlled succession of a certain number of mental operations" whose goal it is "to reconstruct an 'object' in such a way as to manifest thereby the rules of functioning (the 'functions') of this object."[16] Ultimately, structuralism is concerned not

13 R. Barthes, *The Grain of the Voice: Interviews 1962–1980*, trans. L. Coverdale (New York: Hill and Wang, 1985), 115.

14 R. Barthes, "The Structuralist Activity," in *The Structuralists From Marx to Lévi-Strauss*, ed. R. and F. DeGeorge (Garden City, N.Y.: Doubleday, 1972), 149.

15 T.W. Adorno, "Lyric Poetry and Society," *Telos* 20 (Summer 1974): 58.

16 Barthes, "The Structuralist Activity," 149.

with meaning but with the *fabrication* of meaning. Similarly, minimal art replaces essence in art with presence and place: it relies on the void, the space around it, which has been regarded since the Renaissance distinct and separate from the art object. Following the Romanian modernist sculptor Constantin Brancusi, whose *Bird in Space* (1919) treated the pedestal as essential part of the sculpture and affected space as a whole, Minimalist object-based art, by its very definition, affects and interacts with the space it occupies, to the extent that the architectural space surrounding it becomes an intrinsic part of the art. Minimalist sculpture differs from classical and even modernist sculpture by emphasizing the process of viewing rather than the formal integrity of the work and the experience of the work over the composition. The spectator is forced to create meaning from his or her personal experience of the work, which becomes part of the work itself. Minimal art not only invites participation but demands the viewer to share responsibility. The viewer is summoned by the work to responsibility. Barthes called for a historical responsibility of forms; the French ethical philosopher Emmanuel Levinas,[17] for an inspired substitution of the self for the other through responsibility, creating ethical arenas where structuralist and existentialist ideals converge. Barthes and Levinas remind us that the production and the reception of art both are *active* forms of communication and that all matter is "interested."

According to Levinas, who combined the phenomenological concepts of Husserl and Heidegger, transcendence is not a modality of essence – not a question of being or not-being – but rather an ethical imperative; it is not a *safe space* of solipsistic inwardness but a site of responsibility for others.

17 E. Levinas, *Otherwise Than Being, or Beyond Essence*, trans. A. Lingis (Pittsburgh: Duquesne University Press, 1999).

In the transcendental beyond, we are ordered toward responsibility for the other. This responsibility, which Levinas calls the "otherwise than being," substitutes subjectivity (the self of the artist) for another: it becomes the other in the same. Inspired by the other it exists through the other and for the other without losing its original identity:

> If transcendence has meaning, it can only signify the fact that the *event of being*, the *esse*, the *essence*, passes over to what is other than being... Transcendence is passing over to being's *other*, otherwise than being. Not *to be otherwise*, but *otherwise than being*.[18]

The Case of Abraham

FOLLOWING HEGEL'S DESCRIPTION of the creative process as "unhappy consciousness," Kierkegaard writes, "all poet-existence... necessarily must be unhappy."[19] As Mark Rothko sensed correctly from his reading of Kierkegaard, sacrifice is central to the existence of the artist: the artist sacrifices everything at the danger of loosing his authentic existence.

Moralists may be scandalized by the "case" of Abraham who placed himself outside universal law, answering only to God:

> The paradox of faith, then, is this: that the single individual is higher than the universal, that the single individual... determines his relation to the universal by his relation to the absolute,

18 Levinas, *Otherwise Than Being*, 3.
19 Kierkegaard, *Journal and Papers*, 1:369 [800].

> not his relation to the absolute by his relation to the universal.[20]

Called upon by God to perform a crime against universal law, Abraham had to bear his secret alone, in *silence*,[21] even deceiving his wife Sarah, the representative of matriarchal/universal law, who found herself confined to *hysterical* laughter.[22] Abraham could not speak the unspeakable: "Abraham *cannot* speak, because he cannot say that which would explain everything (that is, making

20 S. Kierkegaard, *Fear and Trembling/Repetition*, ed. and trans. H.V. and E.H. Hong (Princeton, N.J.: Princeton University Press, 1983), 70.

21 Kierkegaard chose the pseudonym Johannes de Silentio for the author of *Fear and Trembling*.

22 F. Kafka, "Abraham," in *Parables and Paradoxes* (New York: Schocken, 1958): "It was different for the other Abrahams, who stood in the house they were building and suddenly had to go up on Mount Moriah; it is possible that they did not even have a son, yet already had to sacrifice him. These are impossibilities, and Sarah was right to laugh." (43) Sarah as the representative of the matriarchal law, can only laugh in the face of her own powerlessness. Cf. Kierkegaard, *Repetition*, 143: "When a girl's love is not a sacrificing love, she is not feminine but masculine, and then I shall always give myself the pleasure of letting her incur revenge or laughter."

Avital Ronell offers another interpretation of Sarah's laughter: "There were Abrahams who were called before they were ready, that is, before their houses were readied, much less built. These were pure sacrificial beings who were prepared to surrender that which they did not have. This sacrifice, following the logic of the parable, is greater even than that of Abraham who had someone to give up to a higher power. These Abrahams gave what they could not offer. Hence Sarah laughs at the gift that, never having been given, is already, 'suddenly,' given away and somehow redeemed. She laughs at the peculiar nothingness of the gift, the danger and disruption of the gift that bears no present... Laughing she surrenders an unnameable gift." (A. Ronell, *Stupidity* [Urbana and Chicago: University of Illinois Press, 2002], 289)

it understandable)."[23] As Wittgenstein demonstrated, language cannot make *everything* understandable. Similarly, Mark Rothko considered restraint in communication a necessity for any true artist:

> Another problem of Abraham was whether to tell Sarah. This is a problem of reticence. Some artists want to tell all like at a confessional. I, as a craftsman, prefer to tell little... Silence is so accurate.[24]

Abraham is the Special Individual or *extraordinarius* who finds himself mired in a *tragic collision* of ethics and religion, a dialectical relationship with the universal and the single individual that ends in a "teleological suspension of the ethical":[25]

> When the single individual...wants to renew *the life of the established order by bringing a new point of departure for it, a new point of departure in relation to the basic presupposition of the established order,* when he, by submitting directly to God, must relate himself transformingly to the established order–then he is the extraordinary... His *discrimen* is either to take his extraordinariness in vain as a brilliant difference and cause irreparable confusion or, first and foremost before he considers communicating the whole new view that has dawned on him, to sacrifice himself and thereby reconcile himself with the universal.[26]

23 Kierkegaard, *Fear and Trembling*, 115.

24 Breslin, *Mark Rothko*, 393 (see chap. 2, n. 9).

25 Kierkegaard, *Journals and Papers*, 6:6718.

26 S. Kierkegaard, *The Book on Adler*, ed. and trans H.V. and E.H. Hong (Princeton, N.J.: Princeton University Press, 1998), 149–50, 165.

The Special Individual must be *unconditionally* willing to sacrifice:

> When the single individual actually is the true extraordinary and actually has a new point of departure, when he comprehends his life's distressing difficulty in that *discrimen* between the universal and the singular *extra ordinem*, he must be unconditionally recognizable by his being *willing to bring a sacrifice.*[27]

The sacrifice is situated by Kierkegaard in the in-between of nothingness and anxiety, between the Imaginary and the Symbolic, that which Kierkegaard, writing on the theater, describes in *Repetition* as "disquieting supervision of responsibility."[28] Kierkegaard's concept of anguish became the basis for Sartre's existentialism, which emphasized its ethical significance:

> The existentialists said once that man is anguish. What that means is this: the man who involves himself and who realizes that he is not only the person he chooses to be, but also a lawmaker who is, at the same time, choosing mankind as well as himself, cannot help escape the feeling of his total and deep responsibility... This is the anguish that Kierkegaard called the anguish of Abraham...which is the kind that existentialism describes, is explained...by a

27 Ibid., 154–57.

28 Kierkegaard, *Repetition*, 156. See also G. Pattison, "Art in an Age of Reflection," in *The Cambridge Companion to Kierkegaard*, ed. A. Hannay and G.D. Marino (Cambridge: Cambridge University Press, 1998), 94: "The word 'disquieting' is the Danish *aengstende*, which literally means "causing anxiety."

> direct responsibility to the other men whom it involves.[29]

Abraham is Kierkegaard's paragon of the Extraordinary. His sacrifice is the sacrifice of the Special Individual; his silence is "the dreadful responsibility if he heard or has heard wrong."[30] The responsibility of forms becomes "the horror of the responsibility."[31] His conscience becomes certitude, no longer knowledge, or chatter, but as Heidegger will say, the conscience [*Gewissen*] speaks "in the mode of keeping silent [*im Modus des Schweigens*]."[32]

The Genius and the Apostle

THE SPECIAL INDIVIDUAL is in the anxiety of failure, in "fear and trembling . . . from being in error."[33] He is victorious "whether or not he falls": "His relationship to God is his victory,"[34] while the ordinary "man of movement" is concerned with success, with *not*-failing; because he can never rule out failure he will not leap. The Extraordinary has "eternity's certainty" and thus is equally unconcerned with victory and failure:

> The man of movement has no eternal conviction; therefore, in the eternal sense, he cannot possibly be secure . . . The *telos* of his striving is not only that it will be victorious *but that its being victorious* will basically convince the man

29 J.-P. Sartre, *Existentialism and Human Emotions*, trans. B. Frechtman and H.E. Barnes (New York: Philosophical Library, 1957), 18–19.

30 Kierkegaard, *The Book on Adler*, 154.

31 Ibid.

32 Heidegger, *Being and Time*, par. 56 (see chap. 4, n. 14).

33 Kierkegaard, *The Book on Adler*, 143.

34 Ibid., 161.

> of movement that *he was right*, that his proposal was true . . . He does not have certainty but attains it only when he has been victorious. The true extraordinary, however, has the heterogeneous certainty, has eternity's certainty whether or not he falls.[35]

In *The Book on Adler*, Kierkegaard wrote extensively on Genius and its antagonist, the Apostle. The Danish pastor Adolphe P. Adler initially claimed to have experienced a revelation dictated by Christ but later recanted, stating that his work was instead a product of genius. Kierkegaard asserted that Adler confused the categories of genius and divine revelation, of genius and apostle; the latter being associated with the absolute (the religious) and speaking with (divine) authority:

> What, then, is authority? Is authority the profundity of the doctrine, its excellence, its brilliance? Not at all . . . Authority . . . is something that one cannot acquire by having perfectly understood the doctrine. *Authority is a specific quality that enters from somewhere else and qualitatively asserts itself precisely when the content of the statement or the act is made a matter of indifference aesthetically.*[36]

Kierkegaard, who considered himself merely "a genius in a provincial town,"[37] made a point of saying that he is

35 Ibid., 157–58.

36 Ibid., 179. Cf. Alexander Pushkin's celebration of the poet as a prophetic figure in his 1826 poem *The Prophet*: "Stand Prophet, you are my will./Be my witness. Go/Through all seas and lands. With the Word/Burn the hearts of the people" (trans. Ted Hughes).

37 S. Kierkegaard, *The Point of View*, trans. W. Lowrie (London: Oxford University Press, 1939), 100.

"without authority."[38] Following the Paulinian predilection for the foolish over the wise, Kierkegaard reverses the traditional view of genius by declaring the apostle the *anti-genius* – the exception *sub species aeternitatis* (under the aspect of eternity):

> A genius and an apostle are qualitatively different, are qualifications that belong each in its qualitative sphere: of immanence and of transcendence... [T]he genius can very well have something new to bring, but this in turn vanishes in the human race's general assimilation... The apostle has something paradoxically new to bring, the newness of which, just because it is essentially paradoxical and not an anticipation pertaining to the development of the human race, continually remains... The genius has only immanent teleology; the apostle is absolutely teleologically positioned paradoxically.[39]

Kierkegaard here refers to the traditional definition of genius as merely passive endowment or gift:

> Genius, as the word itself says (*ingenious*, the innate, primitive [*primus*], originality [*origo*], pristineness, etc.) is immediately, natural qualifications; the genius is born. Long before there can be any questions of whether the genius will or will not assign his rare endowment to God, the genius already is and is a genius even if he does not do that.[40]

---

38 S. Kierkegaard, *Crisis in the Life of an Actress*, trans. S. Crites (London: Collins, 1967), 56.

39 Kierkegaard, *The Book on Adler*, 174–75.

40 Ibid., 175.

Kierkegaard's notion of genius is one of temporary exception and paradox (even if it results in the destruction of traditional modes of experience through the *shock* of modernism),[41] while the Apostle is absolute and thus, like the Genius Decision, exists in a qualitatively different dimension – one that can only be attained by a qualitative leap to faith:

> All thinking draws its breath in immanence, whereas the paradox and faith constitute a separate qualitative sphere . . . A genius may be paradoxical in his first communication, but the more he comes to himself the more the paradoxical vanishes.[42]

The Apostle is first and foremost *difference:*

> It is different with an apostle. The word itself [one who is sent, *Greek*] indicates the difference. An apostle is not born; an apostle is a man who is called and appointed by God and sent by him on a mission. An apostle does not develop . . . gradually.[43]

If one substitutes the authority of Kierkegaard's god with the pressing of the Abject, then the Apostle becomes *différAnce*

---

41 See Walter Benjamin's remark on the destruction of traditional modes of experience through the shock effect of the cinema: "By means of its technical structure, the film has taken the physical shock effect out of its wrappers in which Dadaism had, as it were, kept it inside the moral shock effect." ("The Work of Art in the Age of Mechanical Reproduction," in W. Benjamin, *Illuminations: Essays and Reflections*, trans. H. Zohn [New York: Schocken Books, 1968], 238)

42 Kierkegaard, *The Book on Adler*, 175–76.

43 Ibid., 176.

–the exception called upon by the Abject, thus constituting a real and absolute paradox:

> The apostolic calling is a paradoxical fact outside his personal identity as the specific person he is... By this call he does not become more intelligent, he does not acquire more imagination, greater discernment, etc.–not at all: he remains himself but by the paradoxical fact is sent by God... However long it is proclaimed in the world, it remains essentially just as new, just as paradoxical; no immanence can assimilate it.[44]

The paradoxical-ethical relation of the Abject to the artist's decision unto failure, which is based on certitude ("It cannot be thought but only be believed"), is a *qualitative* difference:

> The person called in this way does not, in the relation between persons, relate himself qua human being; he does not relate himself to other people in a quantitative difference (as a genius, an exceptionally gifted person, etc.). No, he relates himself paradoxically by having a specific quality that no immanence can revoke in the likeness of eternity, because it is essentially paradoxical and after thought (not prior to, before thought), against thought.[45]

44 Ibid.
45 Ibid., 181.

Kierkegaard and the Sacrifice of *Jouissance*

KIERKEGAARD'S GENIUS is the inauthentic Extraordinary. Only the *authentic* Extraordinary makes the sacrifice. This sacrifice (the *only* sacrifice–the sacrifice of the Special Individual) is not unlike the sacrifice of *jouissance* that Lacan speaks of: the transition, described in his Mirror Stage, to language and freedom that is only possible in form of a trade-off. Kierkegaard compares coming into adulthood and choosing from various identities to the multiple roles played by actors on a theatrical stage. The succession of personae resembles the "fragmented body-image" in the Mirror Stage:

> There is probably no young person with any imagination who has not at some time been enthralled by the magic of the theater and wished to be swept along into that artificial actuality in order to . . . split himself up into every possible variation of himself.[46]

This "*Schattenspiel* [shadow-play] of the hidden individual"[47] is like the state just prior to the sacrifice of *jouissance*, prior to the knowledge of desire or the "leap" from Paradise:[48] "[It] demands satisfaction, and it is never beneficial to a person if this does not have time to live out its life."[49]

---

46 Kierkegaard, *Repetition*, 154.

47 Ibid., 156.

48 In *The Concept of Anxiety* the leap is defined in terms of the biblical Fall: "Adam's qualitative leap." (S. Kierkegaard, *The Concept of Anxiety*, ed. and trans. R. Thomte [Princeton, N.J.: Princeton University Press, 1980], 39)

49 Kierkegaard, *Repetition*, 154–55.

An even stronger resemblance to a discourse on *jouissance* can be found in the following passage on the "immediate stages of the erotic" in the first volume of *Either/Or*:

> The contradiction in the first stage consisted in the inability of desire to find an object but, without having desired, desire did possess its object, and therefore could not begin desiring. In the second stage, the object appears in its multiplicity; but since desire seeks its object in this multiplicity, in the more profound sense, it has no object, it is still not qualified as desire. In [the third stage], however, desire is absolutely qualified as desire; intensively and extensively, it is the immediate unity of the two previous stages.[50]

Kierkegaard's Active-Passive Leap

IN THE CONFRONTATION between ethical reflection and aesthetical immediacy, the aesthetical and the ethical are suspended in the religious, but not in the Hegelian sense as an aesthetical-ethical "synthesis"; rather, the religious is a qualitative leap. Kierkegaard rejects Hegel's notion of mediation [*Vermittelung*] in favor of a "qualitative dialectic": "It is necessary to always hold the different spheres apart by the use of the qualitative dialectic."[51] The idea of the qualitative leap was not unknown to Hegel.[52] Kierkegaard,

50 Kierkegaard, *Either-Or I*, 84–85.

51 Kierkegaard, *Concluding Unscientific Postscript*, 390.

52 "But just as the first breath drawn by a child after its long, quiet nourishment breaks the gradualness of merely quantitative growth—there is a qualitative leap, and the child is born—so likewise the spirit in its formation matures slowly and quietly into its new shape, dissolving bit by bit the structure of its previous world,

however, dismisses Hegel's leap, which is confined to the area of logic, as insufficient:

> Hegel made use of the leap, but in logic... Hegel's misfortune is exactly that he wants to maintain the new quality and yet does not want to do it, since he wants it in logic, which, as soon as this is recognized, must acquire a different consciousness of itself and of its significance.[53]

But, as Adorno comments, "the real difference from Hegel is not so much the 'leap' but that the 'spheres' do not undergo synthesis."[54] Kierkegaard's theory of the leap as a qualitative transition is broadly aimed at Hegel's "misunderstanding" of the transition to religion as a cumulative, quantitative one, in which something passively "flops over" by "immanental necessity":[55] "Hegel has never done justice to the category of transition."[56] The true qualitative leap is a "movement in place": "To become is a movement from the spot, but to become oneself is a movement in place."[57]

Like Kierkegaard's "echo of irony," which repeats but not entirely reproduces, and the "rotation method" of

---

whose tottering state is only hinted at by isolated symptoms. The frivolity and boredom which unsettle the established order, the vague foreboding of something unknown, these are the heralds of approaching change. The gradual crumbling that left unaltered the face of the whole is cut short by a sunburst which, in one flash, illuminates the features of the new world." (Hegel, *Phenomenology of Spirit*, 6)

53 Kierkegaard, *The Concept of Anxiety*, 30.

54 Adorno, *Kierkegaard*, 90.

55 Kierkegaard, *Journals and Papers*, 3: 21.

56 Kierkegaard, *Journals and Papers*, 1: 110.

57 S. Kierkegaard, *The Sickness Unto Death*, ed. and trans. R. Thomte (Princeton, N.J.: Princeton University Press, 1980), 169.

"remembering and forgetting," the postmodern artist experiences the Mirror Stage again and again. He is the eternal child who repeats the creative act each time *as if for the first time,* like the child who, being shown the crucifixion of Christ for the first time, relives that scene, according to Kierkegaard, "as if it were *this* generation that crucified him... and the child, the first time it hears it, will become anxious and sorrowful, for his parents, for the world, and for himself."[58] The artist, like Kierkegaard's child, is in a *constant state of anxiety.*

Kierkegaard's concept of anxiety is the precondition of his leap to faith. Situating his leap to faith as the qualitative transformation from the aesthetic to the religious, and anxiety in Adam's original sin and man's fall from paradise, anxiety is the *sine qua non* for the leap. As George Pattison remarks, "in *The Concept of Anxiety* itself, that leap is characterized archetypically in terms of the Fall, yet it is also made clear that anxiety may mark the dawn of freedom."[59]

Kierkegaard conjures up Spinoza when he writes that "belief is not a knowledge but an act of freedom, an expression of will."[60] M. Jamie Ferreira regards the leap as the one structural element that informs all of Kierkegaard's philosophies of life.[61] Kierkegaard's leap, often wrongly referred to as a "leap *of* faith" (implying that it is made by faith), is a leap *to* faith, a qualitative transition to religiousness: "the qualitative transition of the leap from unbeliever to

58 S. Kierkegaard, *Training in Christianity*, trans. W. Lowrie (Princeton, N.J.: Princeton University Press, 1972), 175.

59 Pattison, "Art in an Age of Reflection," 95.

60 S. Kierkegaard, *Philosophical Fragments–Johannes Climacus*, ed. and trans. H.V. and E.H. Hong (Princeton, N.J.: Princeton University Press, 1985), 83.

61 M. J. Ferreira, "Faith and the Kierkegaardian Leap," in *The Cambridge Companion to Kierkegaard*, 207.

believer."[62] In Kierkegaard's theory, the Leap forms a structural triad with Anxiety and the Extraordinary; the three notions are intertwined in an existential knot that cannot be separated.

While Kierkegaard opposes the quantitative transition to religion that comes cumulatively and automatically, his leap is not solely an intentional, reflective act. It is neither the passive Hegelian quantitative leap nor a "muscular"[63] leap à la Baron Münchhausen of pulling oneself out of free will. In his *Journals,* Kierkegaard notes that the leap "is essentially at home in the realm of freedom."[64] Yet, Ferreira stresses, in the Kierkegaardian leap this freedom is nonetheless combined with a nonvolitional event.[65] Kierkegaard's leap is decisive but not as a reflective act of free will, through which one selects from several options. Ferreira uses the emerging of a new quality in Gestalt psychology that occurs suddenly rather than gradually at critical thresholds[66] as an analogy for Kierkegaard's understanding of an active-passive leap.

---

62 Ibid.

63 "Not the brute "muscular" will power of a Münchhausen where one closes one's eyes, grabs oneself by the neck . . . and then one stands on the other side." (Kierkegaard, *Concluding Unscientific Postscript,* 99)

64 Kierkegaard, *Journal and Papers,* 3: 20.

65 Ferreira, "Faith and the Kierkegaardian Leap," 216.

66 Ibid., 217–19.

Wheeler's "Delayed-Choice" Experiment and the Collapse of Uncertainty

A BETTER ANALOGY for Kierkegaard's paradoxical conception of an active-passive leap might be John Archibald Wheeler's 1978 "delayed-choice" thought experiment in quantum physics.[67] In quantum mechanics, which describes the behavior of matter and light on an atomic scale, there are two ways in which matter, such as light, can behave: as a particle or as a wave. However, light behaves neither as particle nor as wave; it behaves as *both*. The classical "double-slit" experiment illustrates this paradox, which Wheeler describes as follows:

> A weak source of light sends photons, one at a time, toward an opaque plate that contains a pair of closely spaced slits. Beyond the opaque plate is an array of small detectors that can record the arrival of photons. The detectors produce signals that inform a human observer where each photon arrived... Each photon is governed by laws of probability and behaves like a cloud until it is detected. It passes through both slits, not one or the other, and arrives everywhere at the detector array, with a large probability at arriving at certain detectors, a small probability at arriving at others, and zero probability at arriving at still others. Yet finally, if the detectors are sensitive enough to be triggered by single photons, each photon

67 I first discussed Wheeler's "delayed-choice" experiment in relation to the postmodern in 1987 in the context of the artist Sturtevant. See K. Ottmann, "Elaine Sturtevant," *Flash Art* 137 (November/December 1987), 105–6.

> will be detected somewhere – somewhere quite specific. Where a particular photon will be detected is completely unpredictable. After many photons are detected, the calculated distribution of probability over many detectors can be verified. The act of measurement is the transforming act that collapses uncertainty into certainty.[68]

The result of the experiment presents itself in the form of a paradox: a photon either goes through slit 1 or through slit 2 (behaving like a *particle*) *if* we determine which hole is passed by blocking one of the slits during the experiment. If both holes stay open during the experiment, the photon passes through both slits at once (behaving like a *wave* by creating a pattern of interference), making it impossible for any observer to determine which hole is passed by each photon. This is explained by Heisenberg's Uncertainty Principle, which states that one cannot precisely measure the position and the momentum (mass × velocity) of a particle at the same time: "A photon goes entirely unobserved until it triggers a detector. From the moment of its emission until that moment of detection, one has no knowledge of its location or direction of travel. It remains an ethereal cloud of probability precisely because it is unobserved."[69]

In Wheeler's "delayed-choice" thought experiment, a single light particle or photon is emitted from a light source and encounters a beam splitter in the form of a half-silvered mirror, which acts as a two-slit panel splitting the light into two beams of equal intensity. The split beams

---

68 J. A. Wheeler (with K. Ford), *Geons, Black Holes & Quantum Foam: A Life in Physics* (New York: W.W. Norton, 1998), 331.

69 Ibid., 333.

are directed by the beam splitter toward two fully reflective mirrors–one on the left, the other on the right–which reflect the beams to a crossing point and then toward two arrays of detectors, one on the far left and one on the far right of the experimental field. The detectors determine by which route the photons arrive by measuring the rate of photon hits. In the experiment, a photon appears to go either to the left or to the right, since both detector arrays will have counted about the same average number of hits during repeated runs of the experiment. Then a second half-silvered mirror is installed at the crossing point of both beams, which reflects the light coming from each fully reflective mirror towards the detectors on the far right and left sides. This second mirror is placed in such a way that it will cause a *destructive* interference on one side and a *constructive* interference on the other. A destructive interference cancels out any photons resulting in a photon hit rate of zero, while the constructive interference results in twice the amount of photon hits. Thus the experiment proves that a single photon can take both routes (or pass through both slits) at once. Since the position *and* speed of an atomic particle cannot be measured simultaneously, one can either choose to measure which route a photon follows by running the first experiment, or reveal the interference by placing a second half-silvered mirror at the crossing point (but then can no longer determine which route the photon took).

Wheeler's experiment proves that Heisenberg's Uncertainty Principle can be sidestepped (or cheated)[70] by observing the route choice of the photon after the experiment

70 Slavoj Žižek has called Wheeler's delayed-choice experiment "a kind of ontological 'cheating.'" (Žižek, *The Invisible Remainder*, 226 [see chap. 7, n. 34])

has been completed rather than during its course. If one waits until the photon has left the light source before it reaches the crossing point–about 10 or 20 billionth of a second–before deciding on either measurement (1 or 2), then the photon will already have chosen its route (whether one has inserted the second mirror or not). Thus one decides on the action (route) the photon takes *after* the fact, effectively changing the past by making a decision in the present.

> After the quantum of energy has already gone through the doubly slit screen, a last-instant free choice on our part–we have found–gives at will a double-slit-interference record or a one-slit beam count. Does this result mean that present choice influences past dynamics, in contravention of every formulation of causality? Or does it mean, calculate pedantically and don't ask questions? Neither; the lesson presents itself rather as this, that the past has no existence except as it is recorded in the present... More generally, we would seem forced to say that no phenomenon is a phenomenon until... it is an observed phenomenon. The universe does not "exist, out there," independent of all acts of observation. Instead, it is in some strange sense a participatory universe.[71]

On a cosmic scale, Wheeler's thought experiment leads to the implication that, as observers, humans are actively participating in the creation of reality. Astronomers on earth who observe the light emanating from a quasar, billions of

71 J. A. Wheeler, "The 'Past' and the 'Delayed-Choice' Double-Slit Experiment," in *Mathematical Foundations of Quantum Theory*, ed. A.R. Marlowe (New York: Academy Press, 1978), 41.

light years away, passing through a pair of massive galaxies (functioning as a pair of slits), find themselves in a position similar to the quantum physicist in Wheeler's experiment. They may either point a telescope at one galaxy at a time, or take a photograph of both galaxies and observe an interference pattern that indicates that the light originating from the quasar is passing through both galaxies simultaneously. Thus, even *after* a quasar photon has traveled for billions of years toward earth, an observer can still decide which route the photon took billions of years earlier. Wheeler believes that the universe consists of "clouds of uncertainty," which only become certain or real once they have been observed. Each observation into parts of the universe selects one of many possible quantum histories for the universe. Like the postmodern text, the universe is made up of numerous "writings" with a multiplicity of meanings.

Another key element in Kierkegaard's theory of the leap is the concept of "letting go" (a concept that reappears in Peirce's abductive logic of discovery, in Wittgenstein's *Tractatus* with his ladder analogy, and in Heidegger's *Contributions* as "echo of refusal or non-granting [*Anklang der Verweigerung*]." "How does the existence of God emerge from the demonstration? . . . I have to let go of it,"[72] writes Kierkegaard." The leap is the *reservatio finalis* (the ultimate holding-back).[73] However, this letting-go is not a merely passive

72 Kierkegaard, *Philosophical Fragments*, 42.

73 ". . . anyone who wants to demonstrate the existence of God (in any other sense than elucidating the God-concept and without the *reservatio finalis* [ultimate reservation] that we have pointed out–that the existence itself emerges from the demonstration by a leap) proves something else instead, at times something that perhaps did not even need demonstrating . . ." (Ibid., 43)

condition–it requires the *active contribution* [Zuthat] of the one who leaps. It is essentially *active-passive*:

> ...so long as I am holding on to the demonstration (that is, continue to be the one who is demonstrating), the existence does not emerge, if for no other reason than that I am in the process of demonstrating it, but when I let go of the demonstration, the existence is there. Yet, this letting go, even that is surely something; it is, after all, *meine Zuthat* [my contribution]. Does it not have to be taken into account, this diminutive moment, however brief it is–it does not have to be long, because it is a *leap*.[74]

Just as in the delayed action of Wheeler's experiment the observer temporarily "lets go" of the photons, Kierkegaard's *reservatio finalis* collapses uncertainty into certainty. The stepping-back from the quantum experiment for a billionth of a second is a step towards certainty. Kierkegaard's letting-go is a *stepping back* towards faith.

It should be noted, however, that the delayed-choice cannot be called "retroactive causality." It simply proves that not only the future but the past is undetermined as well. Both past and future consist of probabilities. Similarly, the Nonrepresentable cannot be observed other than as probability. The only certainty is its indetermination. Prior to the implementation of the delayed-choice experiment, quantum physicists were in a similar position as Kierkegaard's "men of movement": Heisenberg's Uncertainty Principle seems to forever preclude knowledge at the quantum level. With the help of Wheeler's ontological ruse, physicists, for the first time, are able to ascertain

74 Ibid., 42–43.

certainty by way of a qualitative leap, not unlike Kierkegaard's decisive leap to faith. The event horizon[75] of the leap is the threshold where uncertainty collapses into certainty. For Kierkegaard, the leap, however brief, is a decisive moment of singularity; one that is active yet passive.[76] Just as in Kierkegaard's leap only the moment of letting go leads to knowledge, in the delayed-choice experiment, only the initial "letting-go" of the photon by the observer can result in the complete knowledge about the photon. As long as the observer is determined to be in on the experiment from the very beginning, that knowledge will forever be elusive. Both Kierkegaard's leap to faith and Wheeler's delayed-choice experiment function, as Lacan notes in speaking of *jouissance*, "on the inverted ladder . . . of desire."[77]

---

75 "The event horizon, the boundary of the region of space-time from which it is not possible to escape, acts rather like a one-way membrane around the black hole: objects . . . can fall through the event horizon into the black hole, but nothing can ever get out of the black hole through the event horizon." (S.W. Hawking, *A Brief History of Time: From the Big Bang to Black Holes* [Toronto: Bantam Books, 1988]: 89)

76 "Aligning the leap, as Climacus does, with letting go already hints at the leap as something curiously active yet passive. Climacus's references to the active dimension of the leap can easily be forgotten in our tendency to see demonstration as compelling us to assent, but in the context of evidence and judgments of adequacy, they belie the notion of leap as a one-sided volitional activity." (Feirreira, "Faith and the Kierkegaardian Leap," 210)

77 "The Subversion of the subject," in Lacan, *Écrits: A Selection*, 324 (see chap. 4, n. 5).

9 / *Nietzsche's Active Aesthetics*

Nietzsche and the Ecstasy of Communication

ELSEWHERE I DEFINED the postmodern, with respect to art, as a synthesis of irony and ecstasy.[1] The historical process that is generally equated with the concept of nihilism and the end of metaphysics (namely the loss of meaning in the modern world) forms a common starting-point for both the modern and the postmodern. While the modern is characterized by a nostalgia for lost meaning, the postmodern is marked by irony and an affirmative ecstasy that resembles Nietzsche's "pessimism of strength":

> Man *no longer* needs a "justification of evil," he loathes exactly the "justifying": he enjoys the evil pure, raw [*cru*], he finds meaningless evil the most interesting.
>
> If he needed a God before, he now delights in a disorder of the world without God, a world of coincidence, of which the horrid, ambiguous, seductive are intrinsic features.[2]

If one interprets Lacan's Mirror Stage as an allegory of the modern, then in the postmodern, as Jean Baudrillard proposes, the deflecting television screen takes the place of the

---

1 See K. Ottmann, *Irony & Ecstasy: Contemporary American Paintings and Drawings*, exh. cat. Salama-Caro Gallery (London, 1993).

2 F. Nietzsche, *Nachlaß*, in *Kritische Studienausgabe* [KSA], ed. G. Colli and M. Montinari (Munich: Deutscher Taschenbuch Verlag, 1999), 12: 10[21] (my translation and hereafter).

reflecting mirror, which is no longer the place of the formation of the subject, but that of its disappearance. This disappearance, according to Baudrillard, can be understood as an ironic strategy of the subject.

In connection with his studies on photography, Barthes speaks of a "photographic ecstasy,"[3] which is associated with a loss, insofar as the photograph is a memory of something that no longer exists as such. The loss, however, does not provoke nostalgia; rather, it manifests itself as an "ecstatic nihilism,"[4] which is celebratory rather than mournful. Barthes describes this loss in *The Pleasure of the Text* as the pleasure of the subject (the reader, spectator, listener) in his disappearance, "the site of the loss, the seam, the cut, the deflation, the dissolve which seizes the subject in the midst of bliss."[5] It is the "ecstasy of the communication," of which Baudrillard writes, with an ironical glance sideways at Lacan: "We no longer participate in the drama of alienation, but are in the ecstasy of communication."[6] It is an ecstasy that becomes "obscene" in the total transparency of the media and computer networks. We now live in a world, in which reality merges with the fictions of television, advertisement, and science. The concepts of the past and future have made way for a permanent present in which all desires become instantaneously fulfilled with the help of the new communication technologies. The task of art is then no longer to invent fictive worlds but to mediate between the audience and these technologies.

---

3 R. Barthes, *The Grain of the Voice*, 352 (see chap. 8, n. 13).

4 Nietzsche, *Nachlaß*, KSA 11: 35[82].

5 R. Barthes, *The Pleasure of the Text*, trans. R. Miller (New York: Hill and Wang, 1975), 7.

6 J. Baudrillard, *The Ecstasy of Communication*, trans. B. and C. Schutze (New York: Semiotext(e), 1988), 22.

The artist replaces, or rather, abolishes the cultural elite as a mediating agent. Kant's mathematical-sublime and dynamic-sublime are joined by a "technical-sublime."[7] The sublime, once the exclusive property of the cultural elite, has become a mass product. On the television screen, violence, sexual fantasies, and psychodramas are delivered safely into people's homes, where one actively and passively participates in talk-shows and Reality TV. Schopenhauer's "eternal world-eye"[8] is as much a camera as it is a camcorder. The technical-sublime becomes the video-sublime, chillingly exemplified in a short story by Don DeLillo, in which a highway shooting is recorded on video through the rear window of the family car by a twelve-year-old girl and replayed over and over:

> Here it comes, all right. He is shot, headshot, and the camera reacts, the child reacts–there is a jolt movement but she keeps on taping... Seeing someone at the moment he dies, dying unexpectedly. This is reason alone to stay fixed to the screen... The horror freezes your soul but this doesn't mean that you want them to stop.[9]

The postmodern reads art as text. The unreadability, the loss of meaning, throws readers back onto themselves and assigns to them an active, central role; only in them will the multiple readings of a work of art come together. Thus Barthes writes,

---

7 See K. Bartels, "Über das Technisch-Erhabene," in *Das Erhabene: Zwischen Grenzerfahrung und Größenwahn*, ed. C. Pries (Weinheim: VCH Verlagsgesellschaft, 1989): 295–316.

8 S. Schopenhauer, *Die Welt als Wille und Vorstellung* (Munich: R. Piper, 1911), 2: 422.

9 D. DeLillo, "Videotape," *Harper's Magazine* (December 1994), 15–17.

> A text is made up of multiple writings, drawn from many cultures and entering into mutual relations of dialogue, parody, contestation, but there is one place where this multiplicity is focused and that place is the reader.[10]

Nietzsche's Active-Reactive Aesthetics

IN DEFIANCE OF the traditional notion of aesthetics as a "science of the senses," Nietzsche sets his "will to power" against the aesthetics of the beautiful and the sublime – an active aesthetics that has to be grasped from the point of creating and producing rather than receiving, that is dealing with the creation rather than the perception of art:

> It is the same here as with the difference between the sexes: one ought not to demand of the artist who gives, that he should become a woman – that he should receive. Our aesthetic hitherto has been a woman's aesthetic [*eine Weibs-Aesthetik*] to the extent that only the receivers of art have formulated their experience of "what is beautiful?" In all philosophy to date the artist is lacking.[11]

In a related fragment Nietzsche asks,

> Does behind the antithesis *classic* and *romantic* not lie hidden the antithesis *active* and *reactive*?[12]

10 R. Barthes, *Image-Music-Text*, trans. S. Heath (New York: Hill and Wang, 1977), 148.

11 Nietzsche, *Nachlaß*, KSA 13: 14 [170].

12 Nietzsche, *Nachlaß*, KSA 12: 9 [112].

In a complete reversal of Hegel's dictum on the end of art, Nietzsche denotes art as the highest mode of Being:

> Art has *more value* than "truth"... the profession of faith, the artist-gospel: "Art as the actual task of life, art as *metaphysical activity.*"[13]

Nietzsche replaces the sublime with an active, participatory aesthetic principle that declares any activity as art and identifies Being as a creative and active state in which each and everyone actively partakes – a world for artists, only for artists, as he writes in the introduction to the *Gay Science*:

> No, if we, who are recovering, still need an art, then it is a different art – a mocking, light, fleeting, divinely unmolested, divinely artificial art, one that blazes up to the cloudless sky like a bright flame! Above all: an art for artists, only for artists![14]

Nietzsche speaks of a "regeneration of art [*Neuschaffung der Kunst*],"[15] accomplished by merging man with "that originary artist [*jenem Urkünstler*]" who is "at once subject and object, poet, actor, and audience."[16] "Man is no longer artist, he has become a work of art," Nietzsche writes in *The Dionysian World View.*[17] In his extended concept of art, wherein all modes of being correspond to that of the artist and the creative process becomes the ruling principle of the universe, Nietzsche grasps the importance of the reconciliation of art and life:

---

13 Nietzsche, *Nachlaß*, KSA 13: 14[21].

14 Nietzsche, *Die fröhliche Wissenschaft*, KSA 3: 351.

15 Nietzsche, *Die Geburt der Tragödie*, KSA 1: 97.

16 Ibid., 47–48.

17 Nietzsche, *Die dionysische Weltanschauung*, KSA 1: 555.

> The work of art where it appears without an artist... The world as a work of art giving birth to itself [*Die Welt als ein sich selbst gebärendes Kunstwerk*].[18]

Heidegger was the first to recognize the active character of Nietzsche's aesthetics:

> This is precisely what is decisive in Nietzsche's conception of art, that he sees it in its essential entirety in terms of the artist. This he does consciously and in explicit opposition to that conception of art which represents it in terms of those who "enjoy" and "experience" it.[19]

Derrida comments,

> Heidegger would have it that, according to Nietzsche, the old aesthetic has never been anything but an aesthetic of passive, receptive consumers. It must therefore be replaced by one of producers...
>
> Stated (or rather translated, since Heidegger doesn't put it in so many words) in another way, there has been, until now, only a philosopher of art. And this philosopher of art, who, face to face with art, never abandons his position in front of art, who never ventures to lay his hands on it, who, even though he at times fancies himself an artist producing works, is content merely to gossip about art.[20]

18 Nietzsche, *Nachlaß*, KSA 12: 2[114].

19 M. Heidegger, *Nietzsche*, 2 vols. (Pfullingen: Verlag Günther Neske, 1961), 1: 83 (my translation).

20 J. Derrida, *Spurs: Nietzsche's Styles*, trans. B. Harlow (Chicago and London: The University of Chicago Press, 1979), 75–76.

Nietzsche's active-passive creative act is a combination of will and instinct:

> What is art? The ability to generate the world of will without will? No. To generate the world of will again without the product wanting to will again. Thus it applies: the generating of that which does not will, through will and instinctively [*Erzeugung des Willenlosen durch Willen und instinktiv*].[21]

In the *Genealogy of Morals*, Nietzsche writes, "There is no 'being' behind doing, effecting, becoming; 'the doer [*der Thäter*]' is merely a fiction added to the doing–the doing is everything [*das Thun ist Alles*]."[22] Werner Hamacher explains,

> that there is supposed to be a doer still behind the doing, a being still behind an effecting, is for Nietzsche nothing more than a grammatical illusion, in which Democritus's doctrine of a undividable basic figure, the atom, is no less caught than Kant's doctrine of a thing in itself [*Ding an sich*].[23]

Nietzsche's model of an active aesthetics belongs with his teaching of an active nihilism to the "experimental philosophy," which does not stop at a "will to the no," the passive nihilism, but accomplishes in the "Dionysian affirmation [*dionysischen Jasagen*]"[24] a revaluation of all values. In his book on Nietzsche, Deleuze stresses the central role

---

21 Nietzsche, *Nachlaß*, KSA 7: 1[47].

22 Nietzsche, *Zur Genealogie der Moral*, KSA 5: 279.

23 *Nietzsche aus Frankreich*, ed. W. Hamacher (Frankfurt am Main: Ullstein, 1986), 5 (my translation).

24 Nietzsche, *Nachlaß*, KSA 13: 16[32].

of the opposition "active-reactive"[25] and the complicity of "action" and "affirmation" in Nietzsche's philosophy:

> This distinction between two kinds of quality is of the greatest importance and it is always found at the center of Nietzsche's philosophy. There is a deep affinity, a complicity, but never a confusion, between action and affirmation, between reaction and negation... Affirmation is not action but the power of becoming active, becoming active personified. Negation is not simple reaction but a becoming reactive.[26]

Nietzsche's affirmative active aesthetics corresponds to his expanded concept of art, which he regards as a "metaphysical activity"[27] and the artist as the "preliminary stage" in a universal aesthetic will-to-power; the artistic subject vanishes in the "work of art that gives birth to itself."[28]

25 "I distinguish between activity and reactivity" (*Nachlaß*, KSA 12:10[111]) and "What is 'passive'? To resist and react... What is 'active'? To grasp for power." (*Nachlaß*, KSA 12:5[64])

26 G. Deleuze, *Nietzsche and Philosophy*, trans. H. Tomlinson (New York: Columbia University Press, 1983), 54.

27 Nietzsche, *Nachlaß*, KSA 13:14[21].

28 Nietzsche, *Nachlaß*, KSA 12:2[114].

The Ur-Eine: Nietzsche's Substratum of Desire

> I? I? I?
> –Ezra Pound

JEAN-LUC NANCY rightly points out, in *The Experience of Freedom*, that Western philosophy led itself to the limit of the ontology of Subjectivity:

> Philosophy... can no longer represent its own beginning as the originary unity of a Subject-of-philosophy appearing to itself in its freedom, or a Subject-of-freedom appearing to itself as philosophy.[29]

Likewise, art can no longer represent its beginning as the originary unity of a Subject-of-art appearing to itself in its freedom. The notion of community as a sense of belonging, *Mitsein*, originally posed by Heidegger in *Time and Being*, lost its credibility in the experience of the Holocaust (being the ultimate Nonrepresentable), and has rightly been dismissed by both Edmond Jabès[30] and Jacques Derrida.

Jean-Luc Nancy attempts a rehabilitation of the notion of community, framing it in terms of Heidegger's distinction between Being-With [*Mitsein*] and Being [*Dasein*], seeing the primary mode of Being as "shared," in the sense of Heidegger's Being-With. But rather than following Nancy's rehabilitation of Heidegger's Being-With, I propose a different

29 J.-L. Nancy, *The Experience of Freedom*, trans. B. McDonald (Stanford University Press, 1993), 7.

30 E. Jabès, *The Book of Questions, Volumes I and II*, trans. R. Waldrop (Hanover: Wesleyan University Press, 1991).

path[31] that would define the aesthetic Self in terms of Nietzsche's notion of the *Ur-Eine* (originary oneness, also spelled *Ureine*):[32] the *Wahrhaft-Seiende* (the genuine Being), which as *Urwiderspruch* (originary contradiction), *ewig-Leidendes* (ever-suffering), and *Urlust* (originary joy), is at once undivided oneness of Being and the *principio individuationis* (the will to self-expression) that causes the Other into Being. It is the Self that is One *and* Other but not One *with* Other). I interpret the *Ur-Eine* as originary pain and joy, like Kristeva's Abject, as a reminder of the original sacrifice of *jouissance* and as such a driving force of Nietzsche's life and philosophy constituting a substratum [*Untergrund*][33] of desire–a sort of subterranean desiring machine. Nietzsche's *Ur-Eine* is a Deleuzian "body without organs." It is "non-desire as well as desire"–a "field of immanence of desire"[34] with no reference to any exterior agency. It is Nietzsche's sacrificial altar of *jouissance*–the eternally split subject.

Nietzsche introduces the notion of the *Ur-Eine* in his "first reevaluation of all values,"[35] *The Birth of Tragedy*. The term *Ur-Eine* does not appear in any of the lectures and unpublished studies preceding *The Birth of Tragedy*, such as *The Dionysian World View* and *Socrates and the Greek Tragedy*. It is informed in part by Schopenhauer's concept of the will as

31 Kindly suggested to me by Friedrich Ulfers during a conversation in Saas-Fee in 1999.

32 Cf. Schelling's use of *Ureinheit* (originary oneness or unity) and its relationship to the Absolute in *Philosophy and Religion*, 23 (see chap. 7, n. 8).

33 Nietzsche, *Die Geburt der Tragödie*, KSA 1: 39. Cf. *Nachlaß*, KSA 7: 8 [7]: "The creative substratum is the Dionysian originary pain [*der dionysische Urschmerz*]."

34 G. Deleuze and F. Guattari, *A Thousand Plateaus: Capitalism & Schizophrenia*, trans. B. Massumi (Minneapolis: University of Minnesota Press, 1987), 149–66.

35 Nietzsche, *Götzen-Dämmerung*, KSA 6: 160.

the primal cause of human existence in *The World as Will and Representation* and in part by Heraclites's action of opposites. In his study on pre-Socratic philosophy, *Philosophy in the Tragic Age of the Greeks* (on which Nietzsche worked concurrently with *The Birth of Tragedy*), he comments on Heraclites's statement that "everything has always its opposite within itself":[36]

> The eternal and exclusive Becoming, the total instability of all reality and actuality, which continually works and becomes and never is, as Heraclites teaches, is an awful and appalling conception . . . It required an astonishing strength to translate this effect into its opposite, into the sublime, into happy astonishment. Heraclites accomplished this through an observation of the proper course of all Becoming and Passing, which he conceived of under the form of polarity, as the divergence of a force into two qualitatively different, opposite actions, striving after reunion. A quality is set continually at variance with itself and separates itself into its opposites: these opposites continually strive again one towards another.[37]

Nietzsche's conception of the *Ur-Eine* put forth in *The Birth of Tragedy* is at first glance merely a variant on the classic Berkeleyan "argument from illusion."[38] Since the empirical reality is only an illusion and we are part of the world

36 Nietzsche, *Die Philosophie im tragischen Zeitalter der Griechen*, KSA 1: 823.

37 Ibid., 823–24.

38 C. McGinn, *The Making of a Philosopher: My Journey Through Twentieth-Century Philosophy* (New York: HarperCollins, 2002), 13.

of illusions, we have no direct access to the genuine Being and *Ur-Eine*:

> In Man [*Im Menschen*], the originary oneness [*Ureine*] looks back at itself through the illusion: the illusion reveals the essence. That is, the Ureine looks at Man, namely Man looking at the illusion, Man looking through the illusions. There is no path to the *Ureine* for Man. He is all illusion.[39]

Nietzsche distinguishes between the naive Apollonian artist who creates the idealized world of representation through form and beauty, and the tragic Dionysian artist who, through tragedy and music, reflects and affirms the primal contradiction and pain of the *Ur-Eine*. The *Ur-Eine* brings forth the empirical world by splitting itself into One and Other, "ever-suffering" from sacrificing its Oneness to the Other. This original sacrifice of *jouissance*, eternally repeated and affirmed by the tragic Dionysian art, goes hand in hand with the Apollonian creation of a mirror world, the representation of a will to self-expression, which only *mirrors* the originary oneness, remaining on the "outside [*Außenseite*][40] of the *Ur-Eine*. Nietzsche's *Ur-Eine* is, like Spinoza's substance,[41] *Deus sive nature*—the ultimate

39 Nietzsche, *Nachlaß*, *KSA* 7:7[170].

40 Ibid., 7:7[161].

41 There appears to be a reference to Spinoza's *amor Dei intellectualis* in the context of the *Ur-Eine* in Nietzsche's *Nachlaß*: "The belief in freedom and responsibility creates now the delusion of the 'good,' that is, the purely willed, the willed without egoism. What now is egoism? Sensation of lust during the individual's expression of force. Opposite: Sensation of lust during the individual's forgoing. Life amongst the many, the lust outside the individual, among the individuals anyhow. To feel one with that which appears is anyhow the aim. That is *love*. The god of the saint is mostly the most ideal

ground of existence and knowledge. Our world of illusions consists of "visions of the *Ur-Eine*."[42] Its essence is contradiction, "thus it can be both the highest ecstasy [*Verzückung*] and highest pain."[43] The *Ur-Eine* is reflected in every layer of empirical reality: "All suffering is *originary suffering* [*Urleiden*], only seen through illusions, localized, in the web of time."[44] Although we have no access to the *Ur-Eine*, we are, as its reflection, part of it:

> Are we at once the one originary Being [*Urwesen*]? At least we cannot find a path to it. But we must be it: and wholly, as it is undividable.[45]

Music is borne out of the Dionysian artist who is "wholly one with the *Ur-Eine*, its pain and contradiction" and "produces the image of that Oneness as music":[46] "The Dionysian, with its originary joy perceived even in pain, is the common womb of birth [*Geburtsschoß*] of music and tragic myth."[47] And thus only music can break through the world of illusions and provide a foreboding sense of the *Ur-Eine*:

> [The] monstrous Dionysian impulse [of the tragic artist] . . . devours his entire world of illusions, in order to let us sense beyond it, and through its

reflection of that which appears and insofar the saint and his god are one. The beautification of appearance is the aim of artists and saints alike; that is, to raise the appearance to a higher power." (KSA 7: 7 [149]; italics added)

42 Nietzsche, *Nachlaß*, KSA 7: 7 [157].

43 Ibid.

44 Ibid.

45 Ibid., 7: 7 [167].

46 Nietzsche, *Die Geburt der Tragödie*, KSA 1: 43–44.

47 Ibid., 152.

> destruction, the highest artistic originary joy [*Urfreude*], in the womb of the *Ur-Eine*.[48]

In his biography on Nietzsche, Rüdiger Safranski stresses the philosopher's existential bond with music: "Nietzsche experiences music as authentic reality and colossal power. Music penetrated the core of his being, and it meant everything to him."[49]

Georges Goedert notes that the ideas developed in *The Birth of Tragedy* continue to have a presence in Nietzsche's later thinking: "In later years Nietzsche likes to fall back to the beginnings of *The Birth of Tragedy* ... For instance, at the end of *The Twilight of the Idols*, he speaks about it explicitly."[50] There, in the last chapter, Nietzsche writes,

> The "Birth of Tragedy" was my first revaluation of all values ... I, the last disciple of the philosopher Dionysus [*Ich, der letzte Jünger des Philosophen Dionysos*], – I, the teacher of the eternal return.[51]

The *Ur-Eine*, in some manner, not only opens "the Olympian magic mountain before us, showing us its very roots,"[52] but Nietzsche's own hidden substratum of suffering and knowledge. The *principio individuationis*, the will to self-expression, is the illusion of the self as Subject. The Apollonian "naive artist" seeks to redeem the originary contradiction with a simulacrum of Oneness:

48 Ibid., 141.

49 R. Safranski, *Nietzsche: A Philosophical Biography*, trans. S. Frisch (New York: W. W. Norton, 2002), 19.

50 G. Goedert, "Nietzsches dionysische Theodizee," in *Schopenhauer, Nietzsche und die Kunst*, Schopenhauer-Studien 4, ed. W. Schirmacher (Wien: Passagen Verlag, 1991), 48.

51 Nietzsche, *Götzen-Dämmerung*, KSA 6: 160.

52 Nietzsche, *Die Geburt der Tragödie*, KSA 1: 35.

> Apollo appears to us once again as the apotheosis of the *principii individuationis,* in whom the eternal goal of the originary Oneness, namely its redemption through illusion, accomplishes itself.[53]

Nietzsche, the Dionysian philosopher, however, seeks to sustain the nonconciliatory, "ever suffering and contradictory"[54] ground of Being. His path of knowledge does not end in the *Aufhebung* (undoing) of the original sacrifice of *jouissance* and the recreation of a Hegelian state of absolute desire, which avoids or bypasses sacrifice at the price of being desireless. For Nietzsche, knowledge is, like "naive" art, an illusion of the *principio individuationis.* It is not the "pure truth without consequences [*reine folgenlose Wahrheit*]"[55] but a series of metaphors:

> We believe that we know something about the things themselves when we speak of trees, colors, snow, and flowers; and yet we possess nothing but metaphors for things.[56]

Understanding is always an ethical-aesthetical act:

> We know nothing of an essence-like quality named "honesty"; we know only numerous individualized, and thus unequal actions, which we equate by omitting the unequal and by then calling them honest actions.[57]

---

53 Ibid., 39.

54 Nietzsche, *Die Philosophie im tragischen Zeitalter der Griechen,* KSA 1: 823–24.

55 Nietzsche, *Ueber Wahrheit und Lüge im aussermoralischen Sinne,* KSA 1: 879.

56 Ibid.

57 Ibid., 880.

Friedrich Ulfers considers the *Ur-Eine* as the source of Nietzsche's "postmodern" ethics, which is "marked by a transcendence of the preservation of the self and of the expectation of reciprocity":

> There is, in Nietzsche's process ontology and in his critique of the generation of moral systems in *Toward a Genealogy of Morals*, a call for an ethics that is not built upon the unchangeability of dominant moral strictures and the universalization that Nietzsche puts into question everywhere he turns his attention on the nature of reality. It certainly follows that, if the conception of the nature of beings is altered, there is reason to seek an alteration in the conception of the relations between beings... Such an ethics is perhaps most closely related to Nietzsche's ontology of the tragic, at the core of which he situates the "Ureine," a "contradiction" in the sense of a primordial chiasmic unity of Being and Non-Being that gives rise to a 'self' which is a simultaneity or duplicity of "is and is not."[58]

In Nietzsche's view, art and philosophy are performative ethical acts driven by the lingering memory of the *Ur-Eine* that presses for an eternal re-enacting of the original sacrifice of *jouissance*. Nietzsche's *Ur-Eine* is related to the notion of "complementarity" that is central to Heisenberg's Uncertainty Principle. For Žižek, the meaning of Heisenberg's Principle goes far beyond simply stating the limitations of the measuring observer:

58 F. Ulfers, "The Idea of 'Bildung' in the Context of Nietzsche's Process Ontology" (unpublished lecture).

> Far from concerning merely the limitation of the observer, its point is, rather, that complementarity is *inscribed into the "thing itself"* – a particle itself, in its "reality," cannot have a fully specified mass and momentum, it can have only one *or* the other... [W]hat first appeared to be an epistemological obstacle turns out to be a property of the thing itself;...that is to say...the very 'ontological' status of the particle.[59]

Similarly, the sacrifice of *jouissance* is inscribed on the *Ur-Eine* itself: the Self of the *Ur-Eine* is One *and* Other but can only be One *or* Other. The absolute selfishness that Nietzsche propagates is the aesthetic Self-that-is-not-One (the "I" of the Artist), an active selfishness evolving out of the *Ur-Eine*. It is always already in relation and therefore inherently, or structurally, an ethical Self, a self that is engaged in an "ethics of ambiguity" and constituted by a decision to failure.[60] Thus the artist has always already chosen to be ethica in order to relive the original sacrifice (no longer Adam's sin but the Promethean-Dionysian will-to-power).

---

59 Žižek, *The Invisible Remainder*, 211.

60 Cf. S. de Beauvoir, *The Ethics of Ambiguity*, trans. B. Frechtman (New York: Philosophical Library, 1948): "From the very beginning, existentialism defined itself as a philosophy of ambiguity. It was by affirming the irreducible character of ambiguity that Kierkegaard opposed himself to Hegel, and it is by ambiguity that...Sartre, in *Being and Nothingness*, fundamentally defined man as that being whose being is not to be, that subjectivity which realizes itself only as a presence in the world, that engaged freedom, that surging of the for-oneself which is immediately given for others... The most optimistic ethics have all begun by emphasizing the element of failure involved in the condition of man; without failure, no ethics." (9–10)

Jean-Luc Nancy requires one to acknowledge that "philosophy and its freedom do not coincide in a subjective presence and that every philosophical *decision* . . . is delivered to itself by something that, unknown to it, has already been raised into thinking." And he continues, "thinking does not appear to itself in a subject, but receives (itself) from a freedom that is not present to it."[61] If Nietzsche's *Ur-Eine* always already carries within its Self the presence of freedom, albeit unknown to it (it is at once absent and present–Lacan's *Fort!Da!*) until it is called upon in the selfish act of communication. (This is not a contradiction as Nietzsche's Self is not a unitary self.) It receives itself from a freedom that is absent yet present–from within the *Ur-Eine* that is One-and-not-One.

Nietzsche's *Wille zur Macht* [will-to-power] can thus be understood, with regard to the *Ur-Eine*, as a *will-to-the-sacrifice-of-jouissance*, which like the Sadean will-to-*jouissance* [*la volonté de jouissance*][62] is ethical in the sense of Kant's imperative. Against Hegel, Nietzsche's will-to-power repeats the originary contradiction and the sacrifice of *jouissance*. Against the Christian notion of *Versöhnung* (reconciliation)[63] of the (passive and "feminine") sin of Adam and Eve, Nietzsche sets the nonconciliatory Heraclitean "eternal suffering" of the *Ur-Eine*–the eternal repetition of Prometheus's *active* sin.[64]

61 Nancy, *The Experience of Freedom*, 8. Cf. Žižek, *The Invisible Remainder*, 173.

62 "Kant avec Sade," in J. Lacan, *Écrits II* (Paris: Éditions du Seuil, 1971), 135.

63 The German *Versöhnung* contains "Sohn," a reference to the Son of God who redeems the sins of mankind by sacrificing himself.

64 Nietzsche, *Die Geburt der Tragödie*, KSA 1: 67–69.

Nietzsche's Apologia for Slavery in the Name of *Jouissance*

FOR NIETZSCHE, the sacrifice of *jouissance* is reflected in the sacrifice, which society has to make for the "good of the highest individuals":[65]

> The happiness of the individual in the state is subordinated to the common good: what does that mean? Not that the minorities are used for the good of the majorities. But that the individual is subordinated to the good of highest individuals... The highest individuals are the creative people.[66]

Their contributions to art, philosophy, and science are directly supported by exploitative labor, not because of their social usefulness but simply because of their superior existence. According to Safranski, "Nietzsche considered the ancient Greek slaveholder society the paragon of culture for

65 Nietzsche, *Nachlaß*, KSA 7: 30 [8].

66 "Now I wish to contrast to the glory of passivity the glory of action, as it irradiates the Prometheus of Aeschylus... The legend of Prometheus is indigenous to the entire community of Aryan races and attests to their talent for profound and tragic vision. In fact, it is not improbable that this myth has the same characteristic importance for the Aryan mind as the myth of the Fall has for the Semitic mind, and that the two myths are related as brother and sister... Man's highest good must be bought with a crime and paid for by the flood of grief and suffering, which the offended divinities visit upon the human race in its noble ambition. An austere notion, this, which by the dignity it confers on crime presents a strange contrast to the Semitic myth of the Fall – a myth that exhibits curiosity, deception, suggestibility, concupiscence, in short a whole series of principally feminine frailties, as the root of all evil. What distinguishes the Aryan conception is a sublime notion of active sin [*die erhabene Ansicht von der activen Sünde*] as the properly Promethean virtue." (Ibid.)

the very reason that it disallowed concessions to the democratic herd animal."[67]

Nietzsche was perfectly aware of the "cruelty"[68] of his view but defended his conviction that the sacrifice of the slave is essential to any artistic development:

> In order to have a broad, deep, and fertile soil for artistic development, the overwhelming majority must be slavishly subjected to the necessities of life in order to serve a minority beyond the measure of its individual needs.[69]

It is, like Prometheus's active sin and Adam's passive sin, an "eternal wound,"[70] one that carries with it a "general guilt."[71] As Safranski notes, "People are sacrificed for the beauty of art, which is why the existence of art adds a further injustice to the wretched state of the world. For this reason, Nietzsche is also prepared to experience guilt in defending slavery, because he is one of those privileged few who enjoy the aesthetic justification of the world. He knows that his own existence is built on the sacrifice of others."[72] Only the Dionysian feast temporarily disposes of all class distinctions: "The slave is a free man, the noble and the ignoble conjoin in the same Bacchic choruses."[73]

---

67 Safranski, *Nietzsche*, 74.

68 Nietzsche, *Der griechische Staat*, KSA 1:768: "If art justifies our existence aesthetically, it does so on the foundation of 'cruelty.'"

69 Ibid., 1:767.

70 Nietzsche, *Die Geburt der Tragödie*, KSA 1: 115.

71 Nietzsche in a letter from 1871, quoted in Safranski, *Nietzsche*, 75.

72 Ibid.

73 Nietzsche, *Die dionysische Weltanschauung*, KSA 1: 555.

Being "on the other side" and ever inaccessible, like the Abject, the *Ur-Eine* is the Nonrepresentable. It can only be glimpsed as a haunting simulacrum in music and tragic art. Here is the link to the postmodern. Nietzsche's philosophy of the *Ur-Eine* is an postmodern affirmation of the impossibility of representing the Nonrepresentable. It is here, in this certainty of failure, where Nietzsche's Dionysian artist and Kierkegaard's Apostle meet:

> On this level of knowledge there are only two ways, the one of the saint and the one of the tragic artist: both have in common that they live on in the brightest knowledge of the nothingness of being without feeling a fissure in their world view. The disgust for living on is felt as a medium for creating, be it now sanctifying or artistic.[74]

Both achieve certainty in the face of uncertainty. When Eric Blondel asks, "With Nietzsche, do we ever emerge from uncertainty?,"[75] one could answer that Nietzsche emerges from uncertainty in the *Ur-Eine*, the One that is One *and* Other. It is here that the Nietzschean uncertainty collapses into certainty, into an ethical-aesthetical certitude that, as Ulfers writes, "would make possible an inherently altruistic relationship, since the partners involved in all relationships, by being singularities – that is, not particulars of a generality or a common denominator – would relate to each other as 'other,' as 'ungleich' (unlike) . . . Nietzsche's dictum to 'live dangerously' could in this ethical context be interpretable not as the recklessness of 'anything goes' but

74 Ibid., 1:570.

75 E. Blondel, *Nietzsche: The Body and Culture*, trans. S. Hand (Stanford: Stanford University Press, 1991), 2.

as the risk one necessarily takes in relating to oneself and the other as 'other,' beyond the certitude of any calculability resulting from 'Gleichsetzung.'"[76]

76 Ulfers, "The Idea of 'Bildung.'"

> $l, \breve{l} \prec \mathfrak{n}$ [i.e., to love and not be loved by implies otherness]
> –C.S. Peirce

THE DISTINCT AMERICAN philosophical tradition known as pragmatism, founded in the late nineteenth century by the American mathematician, philosopher, and logician Charles Sanders Peirce, considered the father of semiotics as a critical theory of representation and interpretation, holds that both the meaning and the truth of any idea is a function of its practical outcome. Fundamental to pragmatism is the conviction that all principles are to be regarded as working hypotheses rather than as metaphysical truths. It was highly influential in America in the first quarter of the twentieth century. Peirce developed it as a theory of meaning in the 1870s, asserting that an intrinsic connection exists between meaning and action – that the meaning of an idea is to be found in its "conceivable sensible effects" and that humans generate belief through their "habits of action."[1] Thus he writes in *Pragmatism as the Logic of Abduction*:

> The elements of every concept enter into logical thought at the gate of perception, and make

1 "The Pragmatic Maxim," *Collected Papers of Charles Sanders Peirce* [CP, cited by paragraph numbers], vols. 1–6: ed. C. Hartshorne and P. Weiss (Cambridge, Mass.: Harvard University Press, 1931–1935); vols. 7–8: ed. A. Burks (Cambridge, Mass.: Harvard University Press, 1958), 5:399.

> their exit at the gate of purposive action; and whatever cannot show its passports at both those two gates is to be arrested as unauthorized by reason."[2]

Peirce's pragmatism is closely connected to his theory of "abduction," which explains scientific and artistic innovation as the outcome of creative processes – an intuitive "fuzzy" logic of discovery unimpeded by rules:

> It is an act of *insight*, although of extremely fallible insight. It is true that the different elements of the hypothesis were in our minds before; but it is the idea of putting together what we had never before dreamed of putting together which flashes the new suggestion before our contemplation.[3]

I regard this intuitive "magic" logic of discovery as the fundamentally American spirit in scientific and artistic innovation, quite distinct from the European concept of *bricolage*. In bricolage, which Claude Lévi-Strauss first applied to define "primitive" science,[4] the universe of the *bricoleur*-artist is closed and the rules of his game are always to make do with *the means at hand*, that is to say, with a finite set of tools. Peirce insisted that abduction, though little hampered by logical rules, nevertheless constitutes logical inference – a *letting go of logic within logic*. Abductive inference arises out of surprising, unexpected, and unexplainable phenomena. The philosopher N.R. Hanson, who widely popularized Peirce's notion of abduction in the 1960s, distinguishes three parts in the logic of discovery:

2 Peirce, "Lecture VII: Pragmatism and Abduction," CP 5: 212.

3 Ibid., 181.

4 C. Lévi-Strauss, *La Pensée sauvage* (Paris: Librairie Plon, 1962).

> 1. [It] proceeds retroductively, from an anomaly to 2. the delineation of a kind of explanatory [hypothesis] which 3. fits into an organized pattern of concepts.[5]

Peirce's abductive thinking is the ontological equivalent of the "magical function of speech"[6] described by the Japanese linguist Toshihiko Izutsu. In his study, Izutsu suggests that all language is essentially magical, "that our words and sentences, before being utilized by professional magicians and sorcerers for their erroneous or evil purposes, are in themselves ultimately of a magical nature."[7] He names three aspects of this linguistic magic:

> (1) The fundamental magic of meaning, that is, the notion of magic which is found embedded in the very semantic constitution of our words. (2) the practice of magic by means of linguistic signs . . . in the narrow, technical sense of the word, e.g., spells and incantations, blessings and curses, oaths, prayers, etc.; and as being between these two, (3) the "spontaneous" magic of intense desire or emotion, which may modify even the most colorless words and particles in a very peculiar way and transform them into in a moment into something charged with mysterious power.[8]

---

5 "Notes Toward a Logic of Discovery," in *Perspectives on Peirce*, ed. R.J. Bernstein (New Haven and London: Yale University Press, 1965), 50.

6 T. Izutsu, *Language and Magic: Studies in the Magical Function of Speech* (Tokyo: The Keio Institute of Philological Studies, 1956).

7 Ibid., 49.

8 Ibid.

Isutsu describes the utterings observed in children's play to bring tangible objects into their minds as well as into their hands. These verbal appeals frequently fail to materialize the desired objects; yet,

> their intangible mental duplicates never fail to do so; whenever a name is called, something shadowy is sure to appear; appear where?; in the mind? or in some other place?[9]

These magic "language-games" are not unlike an version of Peirce's concept of "Pure Play," a form of playful contemplation or reverie that "serves no purpose save casting aside all serious purpose" and "has no rules, except for this very law of liberty." For Peirce, this "*petite bouchée* with the Universes"[10] is what makes discovery and innovation possible.

All works of art that run up against the boundary of representation are endowed with a certain self-revelatory quality, which does not depend on outside references. For Peirce, Firstness is *Possibility*; Secondness, *Presence*; and Thirdness, *Futurity*. Firstness without Secondness is *mere* Possibility. Thirdness involves *Knowledge* and knowledge is *Representation.*

Any work of art possesses Firstness–for example, a red painting. It has the potential of presence. It begins in the artist's studio with the mere possibility of the color red. But it only "exists" when we perceive it. It now exists, but not in itself, no longer as an absolute as no two pairs of eyes see the same red. The color red has left its Possibility and enters Presence, but it only is present for a moment: it is

9 Ibid., 55.

10 Peirce, "A Neglected Argument for the Reality of God," CP6: 458.

standing in the Now. In Peirce's words, "Secondness only is while it actually is."[11] This first, unmediated presence of art accomplishes a temporary suspension of time and place. But as soon as we turn away from it, the painting becomes memory, then certainty and knowledge. Experience is replaced by Interpretation.

Peirce's Evolutionary Love

IN HIS SCIENTIFIC METAPHYSICS, a synthesis of science and theology, Peirce proposed a theory of "Evolutionary Love." Peirce discerns three evolutionary principles: *tychastic* (Chance), *anancastic* (Continuity), and *agapastic* (Love):

> Three modes of evolution have thus been brought before us: evolution by fortuitous variation, evolution by mechanical necessity, and evolution by creative love. We may term them tychastic evolution, or tychasm, anancastic evolution, or anancasm, and agapastic evolution, or agapasm. The doctrines which represent these as severally of principal importance we may term tychasticism, anancasticism, and agapasticism. On the other hand the mere propositions that absolute chance, mechanical necessity, and the law of love are severally operative in the cosmos may receive the names of tychism, anancism, and agapism.[12]

11 *The Essential Peirce*, vol. 2: *Selected Philosophical Writings, 1893–1913*, ed. Peirce Edition Project (Bloomington: Indiana University Press, 1998), 268.

12 Peirce, "Evolutionary Love," CP 6:302.

Following John's "ontological"[13] statement that "God is love," and expanding Darwin's Theory of Evolution, "the greatest mental awakening since Newton and Leibnitz,"[14] to the mind, he constructed the formula for an "evolutionary philosophy,"[15] wherein agapism (creative love) becomes its "central agency":[16]

> All three modes of evolution are composed of the same general elements. Agapism exhibits them the most clearly.[17]

It is this creative love that brings logic into the realm of *jouissance*:

> The philosophy we draw from John's gospel is that this is the way mind develops; and as for the cosmos, only so far as it yet is mind, and so has life, is it capable of further evolution.[18]

Peirce defined agapism on the ethical imperative of "sacrifice your own perfection to the perfection of your neighbor":

> Love is not directed to abstractions but to persons; not to persons we do not know, nor to numbers of people, but to our own dear ones, our family and neighbors. "Our neighbor," we

---

13 Peirce refers to John as "the ontological gospeller." (Ibid., 6:287)

14 Quoted in J. Brent, *Charles Sanders Peirce: A Life* (Bloomington: Indiana University Press, 1988), 60.

15 "The formula of an evolutionary philosophy, which teaches that growth comes only from love, from I will not say self-sacrifice, but from the ardent impulse to fulfill another's highest impulse," Peirce, "Evolutionary Love," CP 6:289.

16 S.M. Harrison, "Introduction to the 1997 Edition," in V.G. Potter, S.J., *Charles S. Peirce: On Norms and Ideals* (New York: Fordham University Press, 1996), xviii.

17 Peirce, "Evolutionary Love," CP 6:303.

18 Ibid., 289.

> remember, is one whom we live near, not locally perhaps but in life and feeling.[19]

Unlike Wittgenstein, who proposed an ethical-aesthetical logic, wherein ethics and aesthetics are inseparable, Peirce assigned ethics to a mediating role between logic and aesthetics.[20]

Peirce contented that triads cannot be reduced to dyadic relationships:

> . . . a triadic relationship cannot be built up from dyadic relationships. Whoever thinks it can so be composed has overlooked the fact that *composition* is itself a triadic relationship, between two (or more) components and the composite whole).[21]

Peirce graphed the triadic relation as a triple fork in "The Simplest Mathematics":

> So prolific is the triad in forms that one may easily conceive that all variety and multiplicity of the universe springs from it, through each of the thousand corpuscles in which an atom of hydrogen consists be but as multiple as all the telescopic heavens, and though our heavens be but such as corpuscle which goes with a thousand others to make an atom of hydrogen of a single molecule of a single cell of a being gazing

19 Ibid., 288.

20 See also R. Kevelson, "The Mediating Role of 'Esthetics' in Charles S. Peirce's Semiotics: Configurations and Space Relations," in *Peirce and Value Theory: On Peircian Ethics and Aesthetics*, ed. H. Parret (Amsterdam: John Benjamins Publishing, 1994), 215–22.

21 Peirce, "Notes on Metaphysics," CP 6: 321.

> through a telescope to a heaven as stupendous to him as ours to us. All springs from the
>
> ⅄
>
> –an emblem of fertility in comparison with which the holy phallus of religion's youth is a poor stick indeed.[22]

Creativity thus becomes a cosmic act–not based on self-love: "For self-love is no love."[23]

As Morris R. Cohen pointed out in the introduction to the first published anthology of Peirce's writings after his death in 1914, *Chance, Love, and Logic,* Peirce's "doctrine of love is not only a cosmologic one, showing how chance feeling generates order or rational diversity through the habit generality or continuity, but it also gives us the meaning of truth in social terms."[24]

Peirce defines ethics as "the study of what ends in action we are deliberately prepared to adopt":

> The ultimately end of action deliberately adopted–that is to say, reasonable adopted–must be a state of things that reasonably recommend itself in itself aside from any ulterior consideration. It must be an admirable ideal, having the only kind of goodness that such an ideal can have; namely, esthetic goodness. From this point of view the morally good appears as a particular species of the esthetically good.[25]

---

22 Peirce, "The Simplest Mathematics," CP 4: 310.

23 Peirce, "Evolutionary Love," CP 6: 287.

24 C.S. Peirce, *Chance, Love, and Logic: Philosophical Essays*, ed. M.R. Cohen (Lincoln and London: University of Nebraska Press, 1998), xxix.

25 Peirce, "The Three Kinds of Goodness," CP 5: 130.

In a manuscript listing nine "Theories of C.S. Peirce 1854," attributed to his future wife Zina, one finds as Theory III: "Love is the foundation of everything desirable or good."[26]

Peirce's radical *logic of love* is based on triadic relationships that go beyond the "me" and "you," beyond "the shock of the non-ego upon us,"[27] from "dyadic relations"[28] to a "special variety of esthetic goodness,"[29] namely, a *cosmically-felt* triadic *expressiveness,*[30] not unlike Nietzsche's *cri de cœur* for cosmic love:

> But not to mistake altruism for its opposite! That would only be love for other alleged individuals! No! To go beyond "me" and "you"! To feel cosmically! [*Kosmisch empfinden!*][31]

26 Theory II defines Genius as being "above reasoning." (Quoted in J. Brent, *Charles Sanders Peirce: A Life* [Bloomington: Indiana University Press, 1998], 51)

27 Letter to William James, June 8, 1903, *CP* 8: 266.

28 Peirce distinguishes eight dyadic existential relations: *extralove, contralove, juxtalove, relove, colove, ultralove, translove,* and finally an absolute *superlove:* "A *super-loves* B; that is, loves whatever may be loved by and something else." ("Dyadic Relations," *CP* 3: 575)

29 Peirce, "The Three Kinds of Goodness," *CP* 5: 136.

30 Ibid., 137.

31 Nietzsche, *Nachlaß,* KSA 11 [7] (see chap. 9, n. 2).

11/ *Wittgenstein's Ethics of Style*

Certitude

THE MOST RADICAL POSITION on certitude is found in Wittgenstein's last body of writings, *On Certainty*, regarded by many to be his third major work,[1] after the *Tractatus* and the *Philosophical Investigations.* It is Wittgenstein's response to G.E. Moore's essays on "common-sense propositions" and Moore's assumption that one can "know" truths that are held to be "certain," i.e., that cannot be doubted. Wittgenstein objects not so much to the assumption of such certainties but to Moore's use of the words "I know." Wittgenstein holds that knowledge and certitude are entirely dissimilar, that there is a difference between saying that one is certain of something and saying that one knows it to be so, if "I know" is meant to imply that it is beyond any doubt, that one cannot be wrong: "The difference between the concept of 'knowing' and the concept of 'being certain' isn't of any great importance at all, except where 'I know' is meant to mean: I *can't* be wrong."[2]

Avrum Stroll stresses that for Wittgenstein the distinction between knowledge and certainty is essential:

---

1 A. Stroll, *Moore and Wittgenstein on Certainty* (Oxford and New York: Oxford University Press, 1994), 5.

2 L. Wittgenstein, *On Certainty*, ed. G.E.M. Anscombe and G.H. von Wright; trans. D. Paul and G.E.M. Anscombe (New York: Harper & Row, 1972), 3.

> In *On Certainty*, Wittgenstein is consistent in distinguishing knowledge from certainty. Knowledge is part of a conceptual system whose other members include guessing, hypothesizing, thinking, believing, and doubting... Certainty... makes the language-game, that is, this set of activities, possible.[3]

But for Moore to say "I know," when there is no doubt, made no sense to Wittgenstein:

> If "I know etc." is conceived as a grammatical proposition, of course the "I" cannot be important. And it properly means "There is no such thing as doubt in this case" or "The expression I do not know makes no sense in this case." And of course it follows from this that "I know" makes no sense either.[4]

It is therefore possible to be in a state of knowledge without being certain and to be certain without having knowledge. Neither requires the other:

> Instead of "I know...," couldn't Moore have said: "It stands fast for me that..." ? And further: "It stands fast for me and many others..."[5]

"Standing fast" [*feststehen*] is one of the terms Wittgenstein used for certitude and must be distinguished from knowing. He identified certitude with *acting*, not with seeing propositions to be true: "Giving grounds, however, justifying the

3 Stroll, *Moore and Wittgenstein on Certainty*, 165.

4 Wittgenstein, *On Certainty*, 10.

5 "Hätte Moore, statt 'Ich weiß...', nicht sagen können 'Es steht für mich fest, daß...'? Ja auch: 'Es steht für mich und viele Andere fest...'" (Ibid., 18)

evidence, comes to an end; – but the end is not certain propositions striking us immediately as true, i.e., it is not a kind of *seeing* on our part; it is our *acting*, which lies at the bottom of the language-game."[6] Stroll adds,

> Wittgenstein italicizes both "seeing" and "acting" in the first passage. He does so in order to delineate certain seminal differences between the concepts of knowledge and certainty: the former is tied to proposition making and has its turf within the language-game, whereas the latter is connected with action and underlies the language-game.[7]

The German *feststehen* implies a certainty without knowledge, while the English translation "standing fast" carries with it the additional meaning of "being in motion," in the sense of Kierkegaard's qualitative leap, which he defined as a "movement *in place*."[8] In his *Vermischte Bemerkungen*, Wittgenstein remarked that "Where others go on ahead, I stay in one place."[9] Might, then, Wittgenstein's activity of "standing fast" be his leap to "faith"?

James Conant quotes from a letter written by Wittgenstein in 1919 to Bertrand Russell that is worthy of Nietzsche's most "nonsensical" aphorisms: "I've written a book called 'Logisch-Philosophische Abhandlung' . . . *Nobody* will understand it; although I believe it's all clear as crystal."[10] It is not

6 Ibid., 28.

7 Stroll, *Moore and Wittgenstein on Certainty*, 7.

8 See chap. 8, n. 57.

9 L. Wittgenstein, *Culture and Value*, trans. P. Winch (Chicago: The University of Chicago Press, 1980), 66.

10 J. Conant, "The Method of the Tractatus," in *From Frege to Wittgenstein: Perspectives on Early Analytic Philosophy*, ed. E.H. Reck (Oxford and New York: Oxford University Press, 2002), 374.

a matter of knowledge but one of certainty. The hermeneutic failure of the *Tractatus* lies not in the reader but in the text itself. That is what the *Tractatus* demonstrates: being "clear as crystal" means the *Tractatus* is "standing fast" in certitude. What, then, is the certain truth of the *Tractatus*?

Wittgenstein concludes the *Tractatus* with the infamous ladder analogy:

> My propositions are elucidatory in this way: he who understands me finally recognizes them as senseless, when he has climbed out through them, on them, over them. (He must so to speak throw away the ladder, after he has climbed up on it.)[11]

This statement seems particularly paradox in light of Wittgenstein's preface to the *Tractatus*:

> The truth of the thoughts communicated here seems to me unassailable and definitive. I am, therefore, of the opinion that the problems have in essentials been finally solved.[12]

Arguably the most "moral" work of logic written since Spinoza's *Ethics*, it encourages its readers to know when to abandon language and logic, and instead trust their imagination: "Whereof we cannot speak, we must be silent."[13] Like Peirce, Wittgenstein proposed *letting go of logic* within logic. As a movement in place, the reader makes a qualitative leap by moving through the propositions of the *Tractatus* without moving at all. It is significant that Wittgenstein

11 L. Wittgenstein, *Tractatus Logico-Philosophicus*, trans. C.K. Ogden (London: Routledge & Kegan Paul Ltd., 1981), 6.54.

12 Ibid., "Preface."

13 Ibid., 7.

chooses the metaphor of a ladder to explain his *Tractatus*. Both Wittgenstein's "ladder" and Kierkegaard's pseudonym chosen for the *Concluding Unscientific Postscript* make reference to John Scholasticus (Johannes Scholasticus Climacus, also known as St. John of Sinai, c. 570–649), the Greek author of the monastic work *Klimax tou Paradeisou* (*The Ladder of Divine Ascent*, translated into Latin in 1583 as *Scala Paradisi*). Divided into thirty "steps," it praises silence, discretion, letting-go of one's thoughts, humility, and dispassion, leading the reader toward incorruption and divine discernment.

The Ladder of Certitude

THE CONCLUSIVE PARAGRAPHS of the *Tractatus* and their implication of ineffable truths have provoked two opposing schools of thought. The so-called traditional view, endorsed by Merrill Hintikka and P.M.S. Hacker, contends that there are certain truths that cannot be said, that can only be "shown" or hinted at by language. By writing "What *can* be shown but *cannot* be said,"[14] Wittgenstein seems to imply a hidden layer of truth that cannot be described in logical propositions but grasped nonetheless: this hidden truth "*shows* itself; it is the mystical."[15]

A second school, represented by Cora Diamond and James Conant, argues that one must take Wittgenstein at his word. Thus no ineffable truths exist. Diamond and Conant oppose the implication that there is a difference between speaking and showing, and instead propose that what Wittgenstein meant by "throwing away the ladder" is to throw away our belief in nonsense or ineffable truths. Conant suggests that "to read the work correctly, we need to hold on to

14 Ibid., 4.1212.
15 Ibid., 6.522.

something and throw something away." He offers for consideration a formalist-structuralist reading: "What we hold on to is the frame of the text – the text's instructions for how to read it and when to throw it away."[16] Thus what we throw away is the content or body of the text.

Wittgenstein's sentence "Whereof we cannot speak, we must be silent" points to an unspeakable discourse of *jouissance*, to a mythical-ethical layer of Wittgenstein's *Tractatus*. Thus there is a third approach that, taking off from a postmodern position by way of his later writings on ethics and certainty, while recognizing the existence of ineffable truths, would not deny a formalist reading of the *Tractatus*. In his *Lecture on Ethics*, which was originally given in German between September of 1929 and December of 1930,[17] Wittgenstein announces from the outset that it is really a lecture on aesthetics:

> I am going to use the term Ethics in a slightly wider sense, in a sense in fact which includes what I believe to be the most essential part of what is generally called Aesthetics.[18]

Ethics and aesthetics constitute, for Wittgenstein, the realm of absolute and ineffable truths, expressed in ethical and religious statements. In his lecture, Wittgenstein dis-

---

16 J. Conant, "Putting Two and Two Together: Kierkegaard, Wittgenstein and the Point of View for Their Work as Authors," in *The Grammar of Religious Belief*, ed. D.Z. Phillips (New York: St. Martins Press, 1996), 286.

17 *Ludwig Wittgenstein und der Wiener Kreis: Gespräche, aufgezeichnet von Friedrich Waismann*, ed. B.F. McGuiness (Frankfurt am Main: Suhrkamp Verlag, 1984), 77n27.

18 "Lecture on Ethics," in L. Wittgenstein, *Philosophical Occasions 1921–1951*, ed. J. Klagge and A. Nordmann (Indianapolis and Cambridge: Hackett Publishing, 1993), 38.

tinguishes between "relative" and "absolute" judgments of value, contending that all statements of fact are, by definition, relative judgments of value while statements of absolute value cannot be expressed in language:

> I at once see clearly, as it were in a flash of light, no only that no description that I can think of would do to describe what I mean by absolute value, but that I would reject every significant description that anybody could possibly suggest, *ab initio*, on the grounds of its significance.[19]

Ethical and religious expressions are in essence "nonsensical":

> I see now that these nonsensical expressions were not nonsensical because I had not yet found the correct expressions, but that their nonsensicality was their very essence.[20]

In a world made up exclusively of statements of fact, ethics and religion are deterritorialized and, like the Abject, *beyond language*:

> For all I wanted to do with them was just to go beyond the world and that is to say beyond significant language. My whole tendency and, I believe, the tendency of all men who ever tried to write or talk Ethics or Religion was to run against the boundaries of language.[21]

19 Ibid., 44.
20 Ibid.
21 Ibid.

Wittgenstein first describes this boundary in the concluding chapters of the *Tractatus* (not yet distinguishing between relative and absolute sense):

> The sense of the world must lie outside the world ... *In* it there is no value—and if there were, it would be of no value.[22]

And he concludes with arguable one his most important statements:

> It is clear that ethics cannot be expressed. Ethics is transcendental. (Ethics and aesthetics are one.)[23]

Art and religion are the realms where ethical statements are expressed as inexpressible:

> There is indeed the inexpressible. This shows itself; it is the mystical.[24]

In Wittgenstein's lecture on ethics, his choice of words, particularly the repeated use of expressions such as "I see clearly," "in a flash of light," "I see now," "I believe" in the absence of expressions like "I know" or "I am of the opinion" (the latter still used in the preface of the *Tractatus*), implies *certitude*, along the lines of his later thinking on the distinction between knowledge and certainty.[25] Using his later text on certainty as guidance may shed light on Wittgenstein's cryptic words in the concluding chapter of the *Tractatus*.

---

22 Wittgenstein, *Tractatus*, 6.41.

23 Ibid., 6.421.

24 Ibid., 6.522.

25 Cf. Wittgenstein's directive "Don't think, but look!" (*Philosophical Investigations*, trans. G.E.M. Anscombe [Oxford: Wiley-Blackwell, 2009], 36 [66])

Wittgenstein uses the ladder analogy to describe nothing other than a *qualitative leap to certainty*. Once the *Tractatus* and its description of the world as the totality of factual statements arrives at the top of the ladder, it finds itself face to face with the boundaries of language[26] – that which is beyond its reach: art and religion, the nonrepresentable and inexpressible. There one becomes aware of the nonsensical substratum of the world and recognizes "in a flash of light" that all sense data have nonsensical counterparts: "He who understands me finally" (who makes the leap into certainty, the *beyond* of language) "recognizes them as senseless" (can experience the *abjected* nonsense layer of all sense). Statements about "the ultimate meaning in life, the absolute good, the absolute valuable"[27] are incompatible with the

26 See Popper on the "problem of demarcation": "The problem which I tried to solve by proposing the criterion of falsifiability was neither a problem of meaningfulness or significance, nor a problem of truth or acceptability. It was a problem of drawing a line . . . between statements, or systems of statements, of the empirical sciences, and all other statements – whether they are of a religious or of a metaphysical character, or simply pseudo-science." (K.R. Popper, "Philosophy of Science: A Personal Report," in *British Philosophy in the Mid-Century: A Cambridge Symposium*, ed. C.A. Maze [London: George Allen Unwin, 1957], 162–63)

Curiously, Wittgenstein is not mentioned anywhere by Popper in this testimonial published in 1957. However, in the footnotes to *The Open Society and Its Enemies*, Popper writes that "the anti-metaphysical theory of meaning in Wittgenstein's *Tractatus*, far from helping to combat metaphysical dogmatism and oracular philosophy, represents a reinforced dogmatism that opens wide the door to the enemy, deeply significant metaphysical nonsense, and throws out, by the same door, the best friend, that is to say, scientific hypothesis." (*Popper Selections*, ed. D. Miller [Princeton, N.J.: Princeton University Press, 1985], 405)

On the legendary animosity between Wittgenstein and Popper, see D. Edmonds and J. Eidinow, *Wittgenstein's Poker: The Story of a Ten-Minute Argument Between Two Great Philosophers* (New York: Ecco, 2001).

27 Wittgenstein, *Philosophical Occasions*, 44.

language of the *Tractatus*; in fact, with any language: "What it says does not add to our knowledge in any sense."[28] Or to paraphrase Wittgenstein, what it does not say adds to our certainty in any *nonsense*.

Wittgenstein introduced ineffable truths into the *Tractatus* because he recognized that while the Nonrepresentable cannot be represented through language, its absence/presence is a necessary truth; as he says at the end of his lecture on ethics: "I would not for my life ridicule it."[29] In a brief synopsis of the lecture, Wittgenstein writes,

> Everything I describe is in the world. In the complete description of the world an ethical sentence is never found.[30]

When Wittgenstein states in the opening sentence of the *Tractatus* that the world is everything that is the case (the *Fall*),[31] he *unknowingly* believes in the existence of an ethical substratum of the world, which is beyond the "totality of facts" and can only be referred to in the form of indirect communication.

For Wittgenstein, as for Spinoza, certainty is an *active* element, the activity of "standing fast" in certainty *sub species aeternitatis*: "Philosophy is not a theory; it is an activity."[32] Thus Diamond and Conant argue rightfully that the *Tractatus* is not about a "result" but about a *method*, about participating in an activity and undergoing an "experience."[33] As Conant writes, "One does not reach the end by arriving at the

28 Ibid.

29 Ibid.

30 *Ludwig Wittgenstein und der Wiener Kreis*, 93 (my translation).

31 See chap. 4, no. 13.

32 "Philosophie ist keine Lehre, sondern eine Tätigkeit." (*Tractatus*, 4.112)

33 Conant, "The Method of the Tractatus," 424.

last page, but by arriving at a certain point in an activity – the point where the elucidation has served its purpose: when the illusion of sense is exploded from within."[34] Conant's conclusion, however, that "the aim of the work is to show us that beyond 'the limits of language' lies not ineffable truth but rather (as the preface cautions) *einfach Unsinn* [simply nonsense],"[35] is unconvincing. In fact, it even contradicts Wittgenstein's announcement in the preface that the truth put forth in the *Tractatus* is "unassailable and definitive."[36] This truth, as his letter to Bertrand Russell testifies, is the crystal clear eye of certitude; it is not a knowledge that can still be doubted.

The strongest evidence in support of the idea of logico-metaphysical ineffabilia in Wittgenstein's *Tractatus* has thus far been presented by P.M.S. Hacker, the dissenting voice among the newer Wittgenstein interpreters. In "Was he trying to whistle it?"[37] Hacker defends this view against what he calls, misleadingly, the "postmodernist" and "deconstructivist" interpretations of Diamond and Conant, by quoting from the following letter, which Wittgenstein wrote to Paul Engelmann in 1917 regarding a poem by the German poet Ludwig Uhland:

> This is how it is: if only you do not try to utter what is unutterable then nothing gets lost. But the unutterable will be – unutterably – contained in what has been uttered.[38]

34 Ibid.

35 Ibid.

36 Wittgenstein, *Tractatus*, 29.

37 P.M.S. Hacker, "Was he trying to whistle it?," in *The New Wittgenstein*, ed. A. Crary and R. Read (London and New York: Routledge, 2000), 382 n5. The title alludes to Wittgenstein's renown expertise at whistling.

38 Ibid., 372.

Hacker comments: "This suggests that [Wittgenstein] took very seriously indeed the idea that there were things that are inexpressible."[39] He goes on by quoting Engelmann who writes regarding this letter,

> I attach immense significance to the way in which [Wittgenstein] formulated his impression [of the poem]. It seems to me indeed that his discovery of what a proposition cannot make explicit because it is manifest in it–in my view the essential core of the *Tractatus* although only adumbrated in the book–has found a lasting expression in this letter.[40]

For Wittgenstein the Nonrepresentable is *contained* in the representable; and nonsense, in sense.

Standing Fast While Running Against the Boundary of Language

WITTGENSTEIN'S *TRACTATUS*, which seems to be modeled in part after the Old Testament and in part after Spinoza's *Ethics*, shows itself as a necessary riddle so that "the *letter* should not be believed more strongly than is proper and the *spirit* may receive its due."[41] These words of Wittgenstein, taken from a comment on Christianity, are preceded by the following:

> Kierkegaard writes: If Christianity were so easy and cozy, why should God in his Scriptures have set Heaven and Earth in motion and threatened

39 Ibid.

40 Ibid.

41 Quoted in *The Wittgenstein Reader*, ed. A. Kenny (Oxford: Blackwell, 2006), 260.

> eternal punishments?–Question: But in that case why is this Scripture so unclear? If we want to warn someone of a terrible danger, do we go about it by telling him a riddle whose solution will be the warning?–But who is to say that the Scripture really is unclear? Isn't it possible that it was essential in this case to "tell a riddle"?[42]

Who is to say that the *Tractatus* really is unclear? Isn't it possible that it was essential for Wittgenstein as well "to tell a riddle"?[43]

For Wittgenstein, philosophy is, like Christianity, "not a doctrine, not . . . a theory about what has happened and will happen to the human soul, but a description of something that actually takes place in human life."[44] Just as Spinoza's *Ethics* ends in the certainty of the *amor Dei intellectualis*, which is no longer knowledge or "sense data," the *Tractatus* ends in the certainty of acknowledging the existence of a Non-representable. What began as a logical *Abhandlung*, in the end reveals itself to be what it is *not*: a practice in *ethics*. If philosophy is an activity, then there needs to be intent for the actions taken. Just as Nietzsche's active-passive aesthetics affirms difference in the primal oneness and the continuous repetition of the original *jouissance*, the immanent activity of *Tractatus* is to demonstrate the existence of

42 Ibid.

43 See also Peirce, "A Guess at the Riddle," his plan for a book on speculative philosophy "with a Vignette of the Sphynx below the Title" (CP 1:354n) in reference to Emerson's poem "The Sphinx," which asks for "The fate of the man-child, / the meaning of man." (J.S. Sheriff, *Charles Peirce's Guess at the Riddle: Grounds for Human Significance* [Bloomington and Indianapolis: Indiana University Press, 1994], 91n6) See also T.H. Whitaker, "The Riddle of Emerson's 'Sphinx,'" *American Literature*, vol. 27, no. 2 (May, 1955), 179–95.

44 Quoted in *The Wittgenstein Reader*, 259.

a Nonrepresentable by *not* demonstrating it–as *reservatio finalis.* To believe in ineffable truths, in a Nonrepresentable within the Representable, and in the certainty of the failure of a complete description of the world in logical propositions, is not a "chickening out,"[45] as Diamond calls it, but, on the contrary, it is the courage of putting oneself in "terrible danger,"[46] in the decision unto failure by recognizing the specter of the original sacrifice of *jouissance*.

For Diamond and Conant, however, the Wittgenstein of the *Tractatus* is the ultimate skeptic. What both fail to see is that the work is really about the *end of doubt*: "Doubting–I might say–has to come to an end somewhere," said Wittgenstein.[47] Even Saul Kripke finds that Wittgenstein was not a skeptic: "Wittgenstein never avows, and almost surely would not avow, the label 'skeptic'... Indeed, he has often appeared to be a 'common-sense' philosopher, anxious to defend our ordinary conceptions and to dissolve traditional

45 "Wittgenstein says, at the end of the book, that anyone who understands him will recognize his sentences as nonsensical after he has used them to get where they tackle you. He must throw away the ladder after he has climbed up it. To chicken out is to pretend to throw away the ladder while standing firmly, or as firmly as one can, on it." (C. Diamond, *The Realist Spirit: Wittgenstein, Philosophy, and the Mind* [Cambridge, Mass.: MIT Press, 1995], 194) See also ibid., 181: "What counts as not chickening out, then is this, roughly: to throw the ladder away is, among other things, to throw away in the end the attempt to take seriously the language of 'features of reality.' To read Wittgenstein himself as not chickening out is to say that it is not, not really, his view that there are features of reality that cannot be put into words but show themselves. What is his view is that that way of talking may be useful or even for a time essential, but it is in the end to be let go of and honestly taken to be real nonsense, plain nonsense, which we are not in the end to think of as corresponding to an ineffable truth."

46 *The Wittgenstein Reader*, 260.

47 Wittgenstein, *Philosophical Occasions*, 377.

philosophical doubts. Is it not Wittgenstein who held that philosophy only states what everyone admits?"[48] While many regard his trope of the ladder as a paradox and riddle, Wittgenstein saw it as crystal clear: "There is nothing *paradoxical* about it,"[49] he states (directed at Kierkegaard).[50]

The intent of the *Tractatus* appears to be a *demonstration* rather than a theory, showing that any attempt at providing a complete description of the world will fail. Just as Kurt Gödel will introduce the certainty of failure into mathematics in his 1931 paper, "On Formally Undecidable Propositions of Principia Mathematica and Related Systems,"[51] Wittgenstein's *Tractatus* brings failure to philosophy (in the form of ineffable truths). What Wittgenstein proves is this: just as mathematical thought can never be free from internal contradictions, so philosophical discourse can never separate sense from nonsense.

There is always a *remainder*, which cannot be put into language or represented as form. Once one undertakes a description of the world within Wittgenstein's framework, one can only arrive at one conclusion: that the propositions of the *Tractatus* are non/sense (sense and nonsense at once) – that every sense data includes nonsensical (i.e.,

---

48 S.A. Kripke, *Wittgenstein On Rules and Private Languages: An Elementary Exposition* (Cambridge, Mass.: Harvard University Press, 1982), 63.

49 *The Wittgenstein Reader*, 299.

50 "The author who seems to have most influenced Wittgenstein's understanding of the category of the religious is Kierkegaard." (J. Conant, "Putting Two and Two Together," 271)

51 "The astounding and melancholy conclusion that the axiomatic method has certain inherent limitations, which rule out the possibility that even the ordinary arithmetic of the integers can ever be fully axiomatized." (E. Nagel and J.R. Newman, *Gödel's Proof* [New York: New York University Press, 1958], 6)

nonrepresentable) data. At that point, the reader no longer "knows" anything.

He *has* to believe: "Now believe!" Wittgenstein tells us, "Believe, through thick and thin, which you can only do as the result of a life–There's nothing paradoxical about that!"[52] Or as in Hamlet's famous last words: "The rest is silence."[53]

For Wittgenstein, sin and sacrifice are always present in philosophy. A revealing anecdote is told by Bertrand Russell:

> [Wittgenstein] used to come to my rooms at midnight, and for hours he would walk back and forwards like a caged tiger. On arrival, he would announce that when he left my rooms he would commit suicide. So, in spite of getting sleepy, I didn't like to turn him out. On one such evening after an hour or two of dead silence, I said to him, "Wittgenstein, are you thinking about logic or about your sins?" "Both," he said, and then reverted to silence.[54]

In a conversation on Heidegger's *Time and Being*, recorded by Friedrich Waismann in 1929, Wittgenstein remarked,

> Man has the drive to run against the boundary of language. For example, think about the wonder at the fact that something exists. Wonder cannot be expressed in form of a question, and

52 *The Wittgenstein Reader*, 261.

53 The later Folio text of *Hamlet* adds "O, o, o, o," the so-called "O-groans." Debated among Shakespeare scholars and editors ever since, they seem to indicate that there is more to silence than one thinks. If the unspeakable can be whistled, perhaps it can be groaned as well.

54 A. J. Ayer, *Wittgenstein* (New York: Random House, 1985), 16.

> there is also no answer. Anything we might say could, a priori, only be nonsense. We nevertheless keep running against the boundary of language. This 'running-against' was seen also by Kierkegaard; he even named it similarly (as a running against the paradox). This running against the boundary of language is ethics... [It] *points to something.*[55]

Ethics, the running against the boundary of language, points to the Nonrepresentable. Wittgenstein's lifelong struggle with the Nonrepresentable establishes him as the first truly *postmodern* philosopher – the first to introduce *failure* into philosophy. (This is not to be confused with *falsifiability*: while the latter is about the *possibility* of failure, the former is about its *certainty*).[56]

55 *Ludwig Wittgenstein und der Wiener Kreis*, 68–69 (my translation). Cf. "Nachwort zu: 'Was ist Metaphysik'": "... the wonder of all wonders, that Being is [*das Wunder aller Wunder, daß Seiendes ist*)." (M. Heidegger, *Holzwege* [Frankfurt am Main: Vittorio Klostermann, 1980], 305 [my translation]])

56 "Falsifiability, or refutability, is a criterion of the scientific status of a theory." (Popper, "Philosophy of Science: A Personal Report," 160)

Ethics and Style

> Style is the general necessity seen *sub specie aeterni.*
> –Ludwig Wittgenstein

WITTGENSTEIN'S FAMOUS DICTUM that "ethics and aesthetics are one" has to be read in the context of his understanding of philosophy as a *living practice.* Ethics includes an aesthetical component, and vice versa.

For Wittgenstein–as for Nietzsche before him–art and morality are closely tied. All aesthetic activity is also ethical, just as philosophy is a practice of life–a *Lebensphilosophie.* It is through *style* that philosophical and aesthetical practices become authentic. Philosophy and art are forms of life: To imagine a language means to imagine a form of life [*Lebensform*]. Language is an activity or a form of life:

> The term "language-*game*" is meant to bring into prominence the fact that the *speaking* of language is part of an *activity,* or of a form of life.[57]

Wittgenstein's note about style that serves as an epigraph to this chapter was written in the 1930s, but is directly related to a remark found in his notebooks of 1915–16:

> The work of art is the object seen *sub specie aeternitatis;* and the good life is the world seen *sub specie aeternitatis.* This is the connection between art and ethics.[58]

---

57 Wittgenstein, *Philosophical Investigations,* 15 [23].

58 L. Wittgenstein, "Tagebücher 1914–1916," in *Werkausgabe in 8 Bänden* (Frankfurt am Main: Suhrkamp Verlag, 1984), 1:178 (October 7, 1916).

Both relate to a reference in Spinoza's *Ethics* to *sub specie aeternitatis* (under the aspect of eternity, i.e., universally and eternally true), which Spinoza links to human freedom. In Part II of his *Ethics*, Spinoza introduces the notion of ideas as active concepts rather than passive perceptions (*at conceptus actionem mentis exprimere videtur*) and ties these active ideas to man's free will (*libera voluntas*).[59] Hegel wrote about Spinoza's *Ethics* that there is "no purer and loftier morality . . . ; the eternal truth is man's sole purpose for his actions."[60]

In a letter to the Austrian publisher Ludwig von Ficker, Wittgenstein writes that the meaning of his *Tractatus* (perhaps the first philosophical self-help book, and the only one based on logic),[61] is "ethical," and that the work consists of two parts–a written and an unwritten one:

> My work consists of two parts: what is on hand and everything I did *not* write. And it is precisely this second part that is most important. The Ethical is quasi defined from within by my book.[62]

Style endows art with soul; style gives it an authentic voice and grounds it in life. In an essay on "Aesthetics and Politics," the archetypal psychologist James Hillman declares that something important is missing from the

---

59 Spinoza, *Ethica*, Pars II, Definitiones III and Propositio XLVIII (see chap. 5, n. 55).

60 G.W.F. Hegel, *Lectures on the History of Philosophy III*, trans. E.S. Haldane and F.H. Simson (Lincoln: University of Nebraska Press, 1995), 275 (translation modified).

61 See Wittgenstein's remark comparing his writing to "a mirror in which my reader can see his own thinking with all its deformities so that, helped in this way, he can put it right." (Wittgenstein, *Culture and Value*, 18)

62 Quoted in M. Frank, *Stil in der Philosophie* (Stuttgart: Reclam, 1992), 88.

political discourse, namely *soul*: "Something psychological is missing."[63] To correct for this deficiency, Hillman proposes an "aesthetic response" that would bring politics and therapy together – a "psychological activism."[64]

Hillman argues that we are aesthetically oppressed, and this aesthetic oppression "affect our bodily feeling, our emotional well-being":

> By suppression of our aesthetic responses, we leave the world to itself and isolate ourselves from its plight. No amount of relating and community building will restore us to the world, and restore the world, unless we trust our aesthetic responses.[65]

For Hillman, as for Wittgenstein, the riddle of life, the riddle that defines the human condition, is an *aesthetical-ethical* riddle that points to the *transcendental* aspect of ethics, which Roland Barthes has referred to as "the responsibility of forms."[66] The riddle does not *exists* because it lies outside the world;[67] it is the repressed: "Ethics not only coopted beauty but repressed it."[68] Aesthetics does not replace ethics, "it give[s] ethics sensate images that direct our longings toward ideals, a vision to contemplate, and seduce towards it."[69]

---

63 "Aesthetics and Politics," in J. Hillman, *City & Soul*, Uniform Edition of the Writings of James Hillman, vol. 2 (Putnam, Conn.: Spring Publications, 2006), 147.

64 Ibid.

65 Ibid., 148.

66 R. Barthes, *The Responsibility of Forms: Critical Essays on Music, Art, and Representation*, trans. R. Howard (Berkeley: University of California Press, 1991).

67 Wittgenstein, *Tractatus*, 6.5.

68 Hillman, "Aesthetics and Politics," 151.

69 Ibid., 152.

Hillman understood that connecting aesthetics with ethics connects us "more profoundly with the cosmos itself":

> How does your own particular aesthetic response connect with the cosmos? To begin with, the Greek word *kosmos* is originally an aesthetic term; . . . [it] means that all things are on display, show themselves, and are presented to the senses . . . Thus your aesthetic responses are cosmological, not merely personal . . . Our aesthetic responses are inherently related to the actual world and to the primary way that we take part in it. To suppress these responses is to cop out of the political, that is, out of the common, shared world. My final point is that ethics alone is not enough to make a change in the world. Alone, ethics without aesthetics doesn't hold . . . beauty evokes *love*.[70]

Hillman refers to this ethical-aesthetical state where the good and the beautiful come together to induce personal and societal well-being with the Greek *kalos kagathos*, an expression composed of two adjectives: *καλός* ("beautiful," "noble") and *ἀγαθός* ("good," "virtuous"). Emmanuel Levinas called this state of ethical beauty "otherwise than being."[71]

Kalos kagathos is evidence of the "soul's active participation in the world," as Hillman writes in a related text.[72] Practiced on a communal level, an aesthetical response evokes

70 Ibid., 153.

71 See chap. 8, n. 17.

72 "Aesthetic Response as Political Action," in Hillman, *City & Soul*, 143.

a Spinozist *active* love, which leads to *ethical care,* and thus to societal well-being:

> An aesthetic perception draws forth our ethical care. First awaken *aisthesis,* breathe in the beauty of the cosmos–the meticulous crawl of an insect, the heave of the frosted earth as winter yields its grip, observe the composite complexity of an ordinary stone, the eddies in the sand as the tide recedes, or hear the early morning bird call. Beauty astounds and pulls the heart's focus toward the object, out of ourselves, out of this human-centered insanity, toward wanting to keep the cosmos there for another spring and another morning. This is the ecological emotion, and it is aesthetic and political at once.[73]

Hillman takes Wittgenstein's notion that any creative practice has to contain an ethical component, and any political activism, an aesthetically component, and gives it a *cosmic* dimension, connecting it to a cosmically-felt sense of beauty that is based on a shared love of and care for the soul of the world.

73 Hillman, "Aesthetics and Politics," 154.

12/ *Heidegger's Last God*

The End of All World Pictures

HEIDEGGER REGARDED the emergence of a "world picture" as the fundamental event of modernity:

> What is a world picture? Obviously a picture of the world. But what does "world" mean here? What does "picture" mean? Here, world serves as a name for what is in its entirety. The name is not limited to the cosmos, to nature. History also belongs to the world . . . World picture, when understood essentially, does not mean a picture of the world but the world conceived and grasped as picture.[1]

In the modern age, humankind has become "subject"– the originator of its own fate. No longer is the world perceived to have been created by an outside divine power, such as the Creator-God depicted in the outer panels of Hieronymus Bosch's *Garden of Earthly Delights*, looking down from above on the third day of Creation at the world below, as it floats inside a crystalline globe. Rather, the world is conceived from within by human self-consciousness. For Heidegger, the foremost manifestation of humanity's new being-as-subject is modern science. During the course of the twentieth century, Quantum Theory and Structuralism

---

1 M. Heidegger, "Die Zeit des Weltbildes," in *Holzwege*, 87 (see chap. 11, n. 55).

became defining powers for representing the world in science and philosophy, respectively; both are likely to do so, at least as long as the so-called unified theory (that combines general relativity with quantum theory) continues to elude theoretical physicists. It is the *failure of the unified theory* that, in effect, signifies the end of all world pictures. Quantum Theory and Structuralism emerged almost simultaneously during the first twenty-six years of the twentieth century (in fact, Saussure's *Course in General Linguistics* of 1916 was published as Einstein finalized the Theory of General Relativity). Quantum Theory introduces the problem of the observer into physics (and therewith the "world picture"). Structuralism focuses on *activity*, on what one *does* rather than on what *is*. Just as former is more concerned with the *experiment* than with its outcome, the latter is concerned with the *fabrication* of meaning rather than meaning itself. Both insist on an immanent analysis located within a system – the universe or a work of art:

> We see, then, why we must speak of a structuralist *activity*: creation or reflection are not, here, an original "impression" of the world, but a veritable fabrication of a world which resembles the first one, not in order to copy it but to render it intelligible.[2]

Barthes cites two principal operations that define structuralism, which also seem applicable to quantum theory: *dissection* and *articulation*. Dissection involves identifying elementary units of a system that, though not actually bearing meaning themselves, are involved in the attribution of meaning, such as letters in a word or particles in quantum physics. Articulation involves recomposing these

2 Barthes, "The Structuralist Activity," 150 (see chap. 8, n. 14).

elementary units into what Barthes calls a simulacrum of the system (a world picture) in order to reveal the rules of their functioning. Quantum physicists call this recomposition the *quantum state* of a system, the construction into which the information we observe about the world is coded. In 1927 Heisenberg published his Uncertainty Principle,[3] which states that it is intrinsically impossible for one observer, located within a system, to give a complete description of that system: a single observer can never view or comprehend more than fifty percent of the world to which he or she belongs. In response, quantum physicists have suggested a community of observers who would be able to collect a *participatory* world picture constituting a multiplicity of world views.[4]

At around the same time, Wittgenstein's *Tractatus* demonstrated that philosophy can never provide a complete description of the world. The impossibility of ever attaining a complete description of the world through a single human or superhuman intelligence is immanent to the concept of the "world picture"–its failure to represent the Nonrepresentable. The modern crisis of representation in art is a direct result of this failure. In *Der Satz vom Grund* Heidegger writes,

> that which is called inappropriately "abstract art" has its legitimate function in the realm of this technical-scientific world construction.[5]

3 W. Heisenberg, "Über den anschaulichen Inhalt der quantentheoretischen Kinematik und Mechanik," *Zeitschrift für Physik*, vol. 43, no. 3-4 (1927), 172–98.

4 See, e.g., L. Smolin, *The Life of the Cosmos* (New York and Oxford: Oxford University Press, 1997).

5 M. Heidegger, *Der Satz vom Grund* (Pfullingen: Günther Neske, 1957), 41 (my translation).

Paradoxically, the possibility of a world picture carries in itself the impossibility of representing the world as picture. The immanence of the Nonrepresentable in any world picture is the *sine qua non* of the postmodern. Modern age placed man at an existential "remoteness of undecidability":[6]

> How far removed from us is the god, the one who designates us founders and creators because they are essential to him?
>
> God is so far removed from us that we are incapable of deciding whether he is moving toward us or away from us.[7]

For Heidegger, there is no substantial difference between the transcendental "Christian" belief in a god (which requires sacrifice) and its "counter-Christian" substitution (which is "only *apparently* unchristian") with "liberal" ideas or "culture" ("for which one does not put one's life on the line"); both are just variations of the same transcendental world view and thus are equally limited by their anthropocentrism.

> As varied as these "world views" are and as vehemently as they openly or covertly attack one another . . . these "world views," unbeknownst and without thinking, all agree on what is already known to be essential to man: that man is the being unto and from which every "transcendence" is determined, and that this is indeed what shall determine him first of all.[8]

6 Heidegger, *Contributions to Philosophy (From Enowning)*, 20 (see chap. 4, n. 3).

7 Ibid., 17 (translation modified).

8 Ibid., 18–19 (translation modified).

In order to free himself or to be "displaced" from the "domination of those 'transcendences' and their mixtures,"[9] man must first experience the "abandonment by being [*Seinsverlassenheit*]."[10] It displaces man into the ambiguity of the *between* [*Zwischen*] that "*en-owns* [*er-eignet*] Dasein to the god," where ownership of *jouissance* is transferred to the god and, at the same time, *jouissance* is enabled as desire for the Other, i.e., for the *gOd*. Here man first recognizes his *jouissance*: "In this enownment, man and god first become 'recognizable' to each other."[11] (Heidegger's *Ereignis*, which is translated in the English edition of *Beiträge zur Philosophie* as "enowning," implies multiple meanings: "ownership of property," "enabling," "appropriation," and "event." It also echoes the meaning of *jouissance* in French divorce law as "enjoyment of property.")

But this "between" is *not* a transcendence; rather it is the opposite, "that openness to which man belongs as the founder and preserver wherein as Da-sein he is en-owned by be-ing [*Seyn*][12] itself–be-ing that holds sway as nothing other than enowning [*Ereignis*]."[13] Only inceptive [*anfängliches*] thinking can leap beyond the domination of the transcendental:

> Finally and above all "enowning" can only be en-thought (forced in front of inceptive thinking) if be-ing itself is grasped as the "between" for the passing of the last god and for Da-sein.

9 Ibid., 19.

10 Ibid.

11 Ibid., 60.

12 Be-ing [*Seyn*] marks the "ontological difference between be-ing and a being" (*Contributions*, 176), the old-German spelling (*Seyn*) signifying the archaicness of be-ing as the unthought dimension within which philosophy originally arose.

13 Heidegger, *Contributions*, 19.

> Enowning owns god over to man in that enowning owns man to god.[14]

Without returning to the place of the original sacrifice (of *jouissance*), to the "hidden reign of the origin of the truth of beings as such,"[15] without "bringing us to ourselves and before the work and the sacrifice,"[16] without experiencing and enduring "the flight of gods"[17] (their accumulation of *jouissance*) and without repositioning oneself in the "*between* "in regard of the self and the Other ("with regard to the passing of the god and the history of man"[18]) at the opening of the "cleavage [*Zerklüftung*],"[19] there can be no "de-cision" and no leap into the extraordinary ("the *non*-ordinary"[20]), no surpassing of transcendence and metaphysics.

When Heidegger writes that "philosophy is useless but at the same time knowing . . . fruitless but rare inquiry into the truth of be-ing . . . grounding of truth while being deprived of what is truth,"[21] he echoes Wittgenstein's *Tractatus*. Not surprisingly, both Heidegger and Wittgenstein share an ontological understanding of the "boundaries of language."[22] In the *Introduction to Metaphysics*, after having already dedicated an entire lecture (*What Is Metaphysics?*) to the discussion of Nothingness, Heidegger writes, "To speak of nothing is illogical . . . Such a speaking about nothing

14 Ibid.
15 Ibid., 41.
16 Ibid., 40
17 Ibid., 20.
18 Ibid.
19 Ibid.
20 Ibid., 77.
21 Ibid., 26.
22 On the many parallels in their thinking, see L. Braver, *Groundless Grounds: A Study of Wittgenstein and Heidegger* (Cambridge, Mass.: MIT Press, 2012).

consists entirely of senseless propositions,"[23] while Wittgenstein states in the *Tractatus*, "My propositions are elucidatory in this way: he who understands me finally recognizes them as senseless."[24]

The Failure of Philosophy

LIKE WITTGENSTEIN'S TRACTATUS, Heidegger's first and second "attempting to overcome the first effort at the question of being"[25]–*Sein und Zeit* (Being and Time) and *Beiträge zur Philosophie (Vom Ereignis)* (Contributions to Philosophy [From Enowning])–are works in process; they are "underway [*unter-wegs*]."[26] While he does not acknowledge the failure of philosophy as resolutely as Wittgenstein, Heidegger puts the success of "the ones to come" far off in the indeterminate future: "Even though the *Contributions to Philosophy* always and only say be-ing's essential sway as enowning, still they are not yet able to join the free jointure of the truth of be-ing out of be-ing *itself*. If this ever succeeds, then the enquivering of be-ing's essential sway will determine the jointure of the work of thinking."[27]

In his *Letter on Humanism*, Heidegger writes about Parmenides's dictum of the certainty of being, which he considers the "inceptual mystery for all thinking."[28]

---

23 M. Heidegger, *Introduction to Metaphysics*, trans. Ralph Manheim (New Haven: Yale University Press, 1959), 23.

24 Wittgenstein, *Tractatus Logico-Philosophicus*, 6.54 (see chap. 11, n. 11).

25 Heidegger, *Contributions*, 176.

26 Ibid.

27 Ibid., 3

28 M. Heidegger, *Wegmarken* (Frankfurt am Main: Vittorio Klostermann, 1978), 331.

> The *esti gar einai* [being certainly is] of Parmenides is still unthought today. In that fact one can measure how things stand with the progress of philosophy. When it attends to its essence, philosophy does not move forward at all. It treads in place in order to ever think the same.[29]

Still, being as Be-ing remains unthought in the *Contributions*. Therein Heidegger distinguishes between philosophy and world view: "World view is always an end, mostly very drawn out and as such never known. Philosophy is always a beginning and requires an overcoming of itself."[30] Like the world picture, world views are "an outgrowth of modernity, a *consequence* of modern metaphysics."[31]

To become the "grounding of the truth of be-ing," philosophy must overcome the modern, distance itself from world views, "take itself back into what it grounds and only build itself up from that."[32] In short, it must become postmodern. (Postmodern here is not understood as simply another "world view" but as a *condition*–the *sine qua non* of the Nonrepresentable. It is not *post* in the sense of one movement succeeding another but, in Lyotard's sense, a *precondition* of any thinking about the Nonrepresentable.) But the overcoming of the modern (the crossing over from *Being and Time* to *Enowning*) is "no gradual development."[33] Rather, it is a (qualitative) leap: "The task is not to surpass beings (transcendence) but to leap over this distinction . . . and to inquire inceptually into be-ing and truth."[34]

---

29 Ibid., 331–32.
30 Heidegger, *Contributions*, 26.
31 Ibid., 27.
32 Ibid.
33 Ibid., 59.
34 Ibid., 177.

Nothingness as Abject

HEIDEGGER'S THINKING after *Being and Time* acknowledges the existence of a Nonrepresentable or "nameless":

> If man is to find once again the nearness of Being, then he must afore learn to exist in the nameless.[35]

The Abject as the Nonrepresentable first enters Heidegger's thinking in his 1929 inaugural lecture *What Is Metaphysics?* in the guise of the "Nothing [*Nichts*]," that which Parmenides categorically excluded from philosophy as the "unthinkable" and "unspeakable."[36]

> What should be examined is the being [*das Seiende*] only and else–nothing [*nichts*]; the being alone and further–nothing; solely the being and over and above–nothing.
>
> What about that Nothing [*Nichts*]? Is it by accident that we speak that way entirely on our own? Is it only a way of speaking–and else nothing?[37]

Jacob Taubes was the first to recognize the ontological significance of Heidegger's transition from the lowercase *nichts* to the uppercase *Nichts*. It is directed explicitly

35 Heidegger, *Wegmarken*, 316.

36 "Either being exists or it does not exist. It has been decided in accordance with necessity to leave the unthinkable, unspeakable path, as this is not the true path." (Parmenides, in *The First Philosophers of Greece*, ed. A. Fairbanks [London: Kegan Paul, Trench, Trübner & Co., 1898], 95)

37 Heidegger, *Wegmarken*, 105 (my translation): "Erforscht werden soll nur das Seiende und sonst–nichts; das Seiende allein und weiter–nichts; das Seiende einzig und darüber hinaus–nichts. / Wie steht es um dieses Nichts? Ist es Zufall, daß wir ganz von selbst so sprechen? Ist es nur so eine Art zu reden–und sonst nichts?"

at Parmenides's dictum that "Nothingness is not" [*medes d'ouk estin*]:[38]

> It seems to me intentionally chosen: with the intent, namely, to reverse the transition from "Nothing [*Nichts*]" to "nothing [*nichts*]," which Parmenides fulfilled paradigmatically for occidental philosophy.[39]

Even Heidegger's choice of words, particularly the prosodic phrase "and else nothing" is an almost literal reference to Aristotle's commentary: "Considering nonentity to have no existence – [Parmenides] thinks entity to be necessarily one, and nothing else."[40]

Heidegger's thinking, like Wittgenstein's, begins with the *wonder* that we *are* (with a simultaneous recognition of the Other): "The grounding-attunement of the first beginning is *deep wonder* that beings are, that man himself is extant, extant in that which *he is not*."[41] Or as he writes in the opening sentence of *Introduction to Metaphysics*: "Why are there beings [*Seiende*] at all instead of nothing? That is the question,"[42] (striking out in the direction of Hamlet's dialectic[43]). But with wonder comes *distress*. The Nonrepresent-

38 Parmenides, *Peri Physeos*, 6.

39 J. Taubes, "Vom Adverb 'nichts' zum Substantiv 'das Nichts,'" in *Von Kult zur Kultur: Bausteine zur einer Kritik der historischen Vernunft* (München: Wilhelm Fink Verlag, 1996), 163.

40 Aristotle, *Metaphysics*, Book I (trans. J.H. M'Mahon).

41 Heidegger, *Contributions*, 32.

42 Heidegger, *Introduction to Metaphysics*, 1.

43 See also Kierkegaard, *Philosophical Fragments*, 41 (see chap. 8, n. 60): "A fly, when it is, has just as much being as the God; with regard to factual being, the stupid comment I write here has just as much being as Spinoza's profundity, for the Hamlet dialectic, to be or not to be, applies to factual being... Everything that exists participates without petty jealousy in being and participates just as

able, and with it man's distress, is grounded in the "cleavage" between himself and the Other – between the Imaginary and the Symbolic. This difference, like Nietzsche's *Ur-Eine*, "belongs to the truth of be-ing itself," and it is "*pressing* ... for the necessity of the highest possibilities."[44] The Nonrepresentable as Nothingness presses for representation. But as Nothing it can only reveal itself rarely and briefly, in the "fundamental disposition [*Grundstimmung*] of anxiety,"[45] of which Heidegger says: "There is always anxiety. It may be asleep, but its breath quivers continuously throughout Being [*Die Angst ist da. Sie schläft nur. Ihr Atem zittert ständig durch das Dasein*]."[46] Anxiety "reveals the Nothing"[47] in the form of the uncanny.

> That in the uncanniness [*Unheimlichkeit*] of anxiety we often try to shatter the empty stillness with indiscriminate talk is only proof for the presence of the Nothing [*für die Gegenwart des Nichts*].[48]

The uncanny, of course, is the unhomely, at once "at home" and "strange" – the "un" standing for the ambiguity of the German *unheimlich* and marking the process of displacement noted by Freud through which the once homely and familiar becomes its negation: the unhomely and unfamiliar – *das Unheimliche*.[49] As Schelling writes in his *Philosophy*

much ... But as soon as I speak ideally about being, I am speaking no longer about being but about essence."

44 Heidegger, *Contributions*, 32.

45 Heidegger, *Wegmarken*, 110.

46 Ibid., 116.

47 Ibid., 111.

48 Ibid., 111–12.

49 Cf. Freud, "Das Unheimliche," *Gesammelte Werke*, 12: 227–68 (see chap. 5, n. 54).

of Mythology, "uncanny [*unheimlich*] is a term for everything that should remain mysterious, hidden, latent, and yet has come to light."[50]

This uncanny is the Abject, familiar and horrifying, forgotten yet pressing from the abandonment of being, "from its place of banishment."[51] It produces at once *anxiety* and *pleasure*. The pleasure it produces is a pleasure of the kind that Freud calls "fore-pleasure [*Vorlust*],"[52] which, like anxiety, is not in relation to a real object but in relation to the Nonrepresentable, and leads to the perception of difference, to unknown, unhomely regions: "In the clear night of the Nothing of anxiety the original openness of the being [*des Seienden*] as such arises: that it is being [*Seiendes*]–and not Nothing [*Nichts*]."[53]

Man is thrown into being as "the thrower [*Werfer*] of being (of the truth of be-ing)."[54]

> The thrown thrower [*der geworfene Werfer*] enacts the first grounding-throw as projecting-open [*Entwurf*] beings unto be-ing.[55]

In this first beginning, "where man first of all takes a stand *in front of* beings,"[56] the distress (the sacrifice of *jouissance*) is still hidden, "covered over."[57] The necessity of philosophy is rooted in "distress."[58] In the *Contributions*, Heidegger

---

50 Schelling, *Philosophie der Mythologie*, SW12: 649 (see chap. 7, n. 3).

51 Kristeva, *Powers of Horror*, 2 (see chap. 4, n. 4).

52 Freud, "Der Witz und seine Beziehung zum Unbewußten," *Gesammelte Werke*, 6: 154.

53 Heidegger, *Wegmarken*, 113.

54 Heidegger, *Contributions*, 32.

55 Ibid.

56 Ibid.

57 Ibid.

58 Ibid.

uses "distress" in place of anxiety. The nothingness echoed in the distress prepares us for the leap, but the leap is rare:

> Original anxiety can awaken in Being [*Dasein*] at any moment. It does not need any non-ordinary event to rouse it . . . It is always ready to leap [*auf dem Sprung*], though it seldom comes to a leap, letting us hover instead.[59]

The De-cision

HEIDEGGER'S PHILOSOPHY, like Kierkegaard's, is a motion in place: "When philosophy attends to its essence it does not make forward strides at all. It remains where it is in order constantly to think the Same."[60]

The Leap itself is described in the *Contributions*:

> The Leap [*Sprung*] (the thrown projecting-open [*der geworfene Entwurf*]) is the enactment of projecting-open the truth of be-ing [*des Entwurfs der Wahrheit des Seyns*] in the sense of shifting into the open, such that the thrower of the projecting-open [*der Werfer des Entwurfs*] experiences itself as thrown [*als geworfener*] – i.e., as en-owned by be-ing [*er-eignet durch das Seyn*].[61]

The leap, which overleaps transcendence, is not a leaping-out but an immanent *active-passive leap* ("the thrower . . . experiences itself as thrown") – a leap *in place*:

59 Heidegger, *Wegmarken*, 117 (my translation).

60 "Letter on Humanism," in M. Heidegger, *Basic Writings*, ed. D.F. Krell (New York: Harper Perennial, 2008), 238.

61 Heidegger, *Contributions*, 169.

> Let us stop here for a moment, as we would to catch our breath before and after a leap. For that is what we are now, men who have leapt, out of the familiar realm of science and even, as we shall see, out of the realm of philosophy. And where have we leapt? Perhaps into an abyss? No!... But on that soil upon which we live and die... A curious, indeed unearthly thing that we must first leap onto the soil on which we really stand.[62]

Von Hermann writes, "This leap, in which transcendence is overleaped, is however not a leaping-out and complete leaving of the transcendental-horizontal viewpoint, but it comes about as *immanent change.*"[63]

The leap, however, is *decisive.* It is preceded by decision–the de-cision [*Ent-scheidung*], separates man from the god by making an in-cision. It "en-owns [*er-eignet*] one another."[64] Although this de-cision is ordinarily thought of as activity or process, "neither the human character... nor the process-dimension is essential."[65] It is not an issue of choice or cause and effect:

> What is called here de-cision, shifts into the innermost swaying mid-point if be-ing itself and then has nothing in common with what we call making a choice... Rather, it says: the very going apart, which divides and in parting lets the en-ownment of precisely this *openness*

62 M. Heidegger, *What Is Called Thinking,* trans. J.G. Gray (New York: Harper & Row, 1968), 41.

63 F.-W. von Hermann, *Wege ins Ereignis* (Frankfurt am Main: Vittorio Klostermann, 1994): 30 (my translation).

64 Heidegger, *Contributions,* 60.

65 Ibid.

> in parting come into play as the clearing for the still un-decided self-sheltering-concealing, man's belongingness to be-ing as founder of be-ing's truth.[66]

The decision is prepared for by the distress – the pressing of the Nonrepresentable: "The preparing of preparation for decision indeed rests in the distress."[67] Without experience of this distress, there is no ground for the decision: "Whoever does not know of *this* distress has no inkling at all of the decisions that are ahead of us."[68] However, everyone is in the decision, even if they don't know it: "Who decides? Everyone, even in not-deciding and not wanting to."[69]

It is not an ordinary decision: "Decision is meant in an exceptional sense, thus also talk of the outermost decision that is simultaneously innermost."[70] It is a decision that is always already decided:

> Decision deals originarily with deciding or not-deciding. But decision means coming face to face with the either-or. Thus it means already *decidedness*.[71]

It is thus a decision unto certainty, an "already knowing" that is beyond questioning:

> *Decision and question:* A more originary enactment of questioning means putting up the essential

66 Ibid., 61.
67 Ibid., 67.
68 Ibid.
69 Ibid., 69.
70 Ibid.
71 Ibid., 70.

> sway of truth for decision. But *truth* itself is already *the very thing to be decided.*[72]

De-cision without choice does not preclude freedom:

> What is this *decision?* [It is] the necessary form of enactment of *freedom.*[73]

We must think of this freedom beyond causality. The decision is enacted in a different time-space dimension, where cause and effect do not apply and where what is important "lies *before* the 'activity' and reaches beyond it":[74]

> The *time-space* character of decision [is] to be grasped being-historical and not *morally-anthropologically*, i.e., as the bursting cleavage of being itself.[75]

The answer to the questioning: the object of the decision is already given; its truth is there before the decision is made. The decision is the leap into be-ing as enowning:

> One thing is decisive here: the leap into be-ing as enowning; and *only* from *this* does the cleavage open up. But this very leap needs the most extended preparation, and this includes the *complete disengagement* from being as beingness.[76]

It requires that one leaves being for Nothingness–the representable for the Nonrepresentable. The leap is a leaping over modernity–a leap into the postmodern as the originary realm of the Nonrepresentable:

72 Ibid.
73 Ibid., 71.
74 Ibid.
75 Ibid.
76 Ibid., 196.

> What is essential to the decision is determined by what is essential to crossing from modernity into what is other than modernity.[77]

The leap will be made by "the ones to come," the single ones – the extraordinary ones who "belong to the last god."[78] Here, in the enownment, which "owns god over to man in that enowning owns man to god,"[79] the passive absence (of the Nonrepresentable) becomes *active* "non-granting":

> This is something essentially other than mere absence. Not-granting as belonging to enowning can be experienced only out of the more originary essential sway of be-ing, as it lights up in the thinking of the other beginning.
>
> *Non-granting* as nearness of the un-avertable makes Da-*sein* the one who is overcome; that is to say: not-granting does not crush Da-sein, but lifts it up into grounding its freedom.[80]

By refusing, by not-granting or, in Kierkegaard's words, by "letting-go," the "utmost remoteness" of the Nonrepresentable (i.e., the last god) becomes a "unique kind of nearness, a relation that dare not be distorted and abolished by any 'dialectic.'"[81] As with Kierkegaard's theory of the leap, there is no dialectical resolve: "Here no redemption takes place."[82] The non-granting prepares the "grounding of truth,"[83] the recognition of the Nonrepresentable as the certainty of failure.

---

77 Ibid., 63 (translation modified).
78 Ibid., 280.
79 Ibid., 19.
80 Ibid., 289–90.
81 Ibid., 290.
82 Ibid., 290–91.
83 Ibid., 290.

PART III: CONCLUSION

Sturtevant, *Johns Device Circle*, 1987
Encaustic and collage on canvas

13 / *The Question of the Postmodern*

Same is a copy, but it's not the same.
–Sturtevant

THERE IS A SCENE in Kafka's *The Trial*, in which the protagonist, Josef K. meets an artist who paints multiple "original" copies of a single landscape painting:

> The painter dragged a pile of unframed canvases from under the bed... "A heathscape," said the painter, handing K. the picture. It showed two feeble trees standing far apart from each other in the dark grass. In the background was a many-hued sunset. "Beautiful," said K., "I'll buy it." K.'s curtness had been unthinking and so he was glad when the painter, instead of being offended, lifted another canvas from the floor. "Here's the companion picture," he said. It might have been intended as a companion picture, but there was not the slightest difference between it and the first, here were the two trees, here the grass, and there the sunset. But K. could have cared less. "They're beautiful landscapes," he said. "I'll buy both of them and hang them up in my office." "You seem to like the subject," said the painter, pulling out a third canvas. "As it happens, I have another similar picture." But it was not merely

> similar, it was in fact exactly the same old heathscape.[1]

The artist Sturtevant[2] produced just such "original" copies of art since the early 1960s by remaking well-known works by exclusively male artists; among others, Marcel Duchamp, Robert Gober, Félix González-Torres, Jasper Johns, Anselm Kiefer, Frank Stella, and Andy Warhol. Her first solo show in 1965 included "copies" of Warhol's *Flowers*, a Johns *Flag*, and a Stella concentric painting. Sturtevant created her works usually just after the "originals" were made, using the same materials and techniques. Her works violate the prime directive of modernism: "Be Original!" Moreover, she did not permit her works to be considered duplicates, copies, simulacra, clones, or fakes. She persisted in pointing out that her paintings were not copies and must be seen on their/her own terms.

In Sturtevant's work, the particle-wave paradox of quantum physics seems to replay itself. The painting *Device Circle* (itself an ironic statement on art by Johns) is by Jasper Johns *or* by Sturtevant, but it is never by both. As Wheeler's delayed-choice experiment proves, the past only exists when it is recorded in the present. Here the foundations of Quantum Theory and Simulationism converge: "The real is not only what can be reproduced, but that which is always already reproduced."[3] *Device Circle* exists only as it is created by Johns or as it is created by Sturtevant. Just as the electron is brought into being by the experiments that the observer chooses to make, so the paintings and sculptures

---

1 F. Kafka, *Gesammelte Werke in zwölf Bänden*, ed. H.-G. Koch (Frankfurt am Main: Fischer Taschenbuch Verlag, 1994), 3:171–72 (my translation).

2 The artist Elaine Sturtevant only used her last name.

3 J. Baudrillard, *Simulations* (New York: Semiotext(e), 1983), 146.

by Johns, Warhol, or Stella are recreated by Sturtevant as "phenomena" in the sense that they are pure Sturtevants.

They prove the truth of Simulationism, which states that the reproduction is the original. Toward the end of her life, Sturtevant had begun to make "copies without origins,"[4] thus pushing the paradox of originality even further. As representation, Sturtevant's works are *failures* (insofar as the leap from image to concept eliminates representation), but as such they are postmodern *par excellence.*

4 In 1999 Sturtevant gave a lecture at Harvard University entitled *Copy Without Origins: Self As Disappearance.*

The dialectic of the modern is largely that it wants to shake off its illusoriness like an animal trying to shake off its antlers . . . Art is indeed indefinitely difficult in that it must transcend its concept in order to fulfill it; yet in this process where it comes to resemble *realia* it assimilates itself to that reification against which it protests . . .

The ineffability of illusion prevents the solution of the antinomy of aesthetic semblance by means of a concept of absolute appearance. Semblance, which heralds the ineffable, does not literally make artworks epiphanies, however difficult it may be for genuine aesthetic experience not to trust that the absolute is present in authentic artworks . . .

That whereby art becomes an unfolding of truth is, at the same time, its cardinal sin, from which it cannot absolve itself. Art drags this sin along with it because it acts as if absolution has been bestowed on it.

–Theodor W. Adorno

14 / *The Antinomy of Aesthetic Semblance and the Paradox of the Genius Decision*

ADORNO DEMANDED that any adequate aesthetic theory must find a comprehensive resolution of the conflict between autonomy and sovereignty that is inherent in modern art—what he called "the antinomy of aesthetic semblance [*die Antinomie des ästhetischen Scheins*]"[1]—without subordinating one to the other. The autonomy of art (and the aesthetic decision) has become a mainstay of Modernism and the concept of the avant-garde. It has risen out of the crisis of semblance. It claims autonomy by refusing aesthetic semblance and denying that in art "the Absolute is present."[2]

Does the Genius Decision resolve the conflict between autonomy and sovereignty? Perhaps in the same way as Wheeler "solved" the problem of undecidability for quantum physics, and Heidegger the "existence" of Nothingness for metaphysics: by way of an *ontological ruse*[3] that recognizes the existence of the Nonrepresentable as a probability that can only be represented as such by *cheating* the aesthetic decision of its autonomy. Similar to Plato's "paradox of freedom," which occurs when the free will of the people is to be

---

1 T.W. Adorno, *Aesthetic Theory*, trans. R. Hullot-Kentor (Minneapolis: University of Minnesota Press, 1997), 103.

2 Ibid. Cf. C. Menke, *The Sovereignty of Art: Aesthetic Negativity in Adorno and Derrida*, trans. N. Solomon (Cambridge, Mass.: MIT Press, 1999).

3 In "The Elimination of Metaphysics through Logical Analysis of Language," Rudolf Carnap accused Heidegger of playing an ontological trick. See *Logical Positivism*, ed. A.J. Ayer (New York: The Free Press, 1959), 60–81.

ruled by a tyrant, the artist in the Genius Decision decides to yield his freedom to the pressing of the Abject. "All theories of sovereignty are paradoxical," writes Karl Popper.[4]

As the world is perceived to be nonobjectifiable, it nevertheless presses to be represented. The Abject/Nonrepresentable presses for a decision; but this decision is not a question of choice. The calling of the Abject/Nonrepresentable cannot be rejected; however, it might not be heard. The pianist Alfred Brendel once remarked that "listen" is an anagram of "silent."[5] Both need to come together; if one does not listen, one will not hear the silence.[6] Hegel's infamous dictum about the "end of art" signifies art's liberation from religion. The birth of autonomous art, which only represents itself *as itself*, is no longer the realm where the divine appears. If Hegel's assertion, which denies spiritual art to be autonomous, were true, how would he explain the global admiration for the formal qualities of African or Asian religious art or the spirituality of modern, nonobjective painting? Perhaps it is not so much a question of autonomous (abstract) art versus non-autonomous (religious/figurative) art, but whether art is endowed with the pressing of the Nonrepresentable (whose representation by definition must always fail) or concedes to the mere presentation of the representable?

---

4 K.R. Popper, "The Paradoxes of Sovereignty," in *Popper Selections*, 323 (see chap. 11, n. 27).

5 Quoted in "Audience of One," in A. Alvarez, *Where Did It All Go Right* (London: Bloomsbury, 2002), 346.

6 Cf. the *Symphonie Monoton Silence* (Monotone-Silence Symphony), a musical composition created by the French artist Yves Klein in 1947–48, which consists of 20 minutes of a sustained single tone followed by 20 minutes of absolute silence. See K. Ottmann, *Yves Klein By Himself: His Life and Thought* (Paris: Éditions Dilecta, 2010), 206.

This investigation argues that the postmodern artist, who is pressed by the Abject into a decision unto failure, makes an autonomous choice precisely by *abolishing autonomy* and does so by deciding *after the leap has already been accomplished.* The paradox of the Genius Decision is that it is a *decision without intentionality*; yet, it precludes the possibility of intervention by an outside power or predetermined fate. Thus the extraordinary is achieved neither passively (by birth or knowledge) nor actively (by intention) but *knowingly* by deciding to do the impossible, i.e., to represent the Nonrepresentable. It is a decision that once the calling of the Abject is heard cannot be refused, and is made in *certain* knowledge of failure. The Modern makes the Abject representable by turning content into form. The Postmodern eliminates content *and* form, thus exposing the Abject as the failure of representation. Finally, the anti-modern aestheticizes the Abject.[7] Only a decision unto failure is a postmodern decision, as failure is immanent in the definition of the postmodern. (Otherwise it would be modern or anti-modern.) As the narrator in Thomas Mann's *Doctor Faustus* says, "There is always a faint, sinister connection between [genius] and the nether world . . . even when it is a matter of a pure and authentic genius, bestowed or perhaps inflicted by God, rather than acquired . . . the fruition of some horrible pact."[8]

---

7 Such as the national-aestheticism of Nazi Germany or the writings of Céline. See P. Lacoue-Labarthe, *La fiction du politique* (Paris: Christian Bourgeois, 1990) and my "Heidegger, Beuys, and the Consequences," in K. Ottmann, *Thought Through My Eyes*, 122–27 (see chap. 5, n. 57).

8 T. Mann, *Doctor Faustus: The Life of the German Composer Adrian Leverkühn As Told By a Friend*, trans. J. E. Woods (New York: Vintage, 1999), 6–7.

The question initially put forth was that of Genius. Asked about in this question was the Extraordinary. In the question of the Extraordinary, the Postmodern has been postulated. The Genius Decision is constituted by the condition of the Postmodern. The Postmodern Condition adds a new variant to the notion of genius that is exclusive to the Postmodern and centers on the question of representing the Nonrepresentable—a representation that can *only* result in the *failure* of artistic production and in a *crisis* of aesthetic reception. The Genius Decision differs from both physical and accidental genius in that it is an active-passive event within the certainty of *failure*. It suggests then that the Postmodern *is* the Extraordinary. But this does not mean that everything that currently falls under the label of postmodernism is extraordinary; nor does it imply that everyone is an artist. Rather, it suggests that a redefinition of the Postmodern may be in order: one that views the Extraordinary in terms of the Nonrepresentable as an active-passive event of failure and considers art "as one of the conditions of human life."[9]

Thus, at last, the Question of Art is called upon.

9 L. Tolstoy, *What Is Art*, trans. Aylmer Maude (New York: Funk & Wagnalls Company, 1904), 47.

15/ *The Question of Art*

> Pleasure and distress, fear and courage, desire and aversion, where have these affections and experiences their seat?
> –Plotinus

> Each of us is compelled by nature to seek an absolute.
> –F.W.J. Schelling

PHILOSOPHERS, SCIENTISTS, AND ARTISTS seek to understand life at its deepest level. Focusing philosophy on the areas of knowledge, duty, and destiny, Kant once defined his objective as providing answers to three questions: "What can I know? What ought I to do? What may I hope for?"[1] These questions are also at the core of every religion, philosophy, scientific research, and creative expression. What unites all of these various disciplines is the quest for meaningful answers needed to create an ethical ground for one's life. Some seek these answers in meditation or prayer, others in political or humanist activities, while still others find happiness in material quests. Whatever answers are found, they all have one thing in common: ultimately, we realize that, as Wittgenstein said, we are always running against the boundary of language.[2]

---

1 I. Kant, *Critique of Pure Reason*, trans. Norman Kemp Smith (New York: St. Martin's Press, 1965), 635 (B 833). See also Peirce's version: "What am I to do, what am I to aim at, what am I after?" (CP 2: 198)

2 See chap. 11, n. 55.

We might call this boundary the nonrepresentable, the indefinite, or the Absolute. Thus the Question of Art is the Question of Life and Death.

Art is defined by life-and-death decisions. As the art historian T.J. Clarke wrote in his study on Nicolas Poussin's painting *Landscape with a Man Killed by a Snake* (1648): "Painting at its most intense revels in its deathliness."[3]

Both life and art are haunted by the presence of *le réveil mortel*, the persistent "wake-up call to death," which the novelist Julian Barnes describes as

> being in an unfamiliar hotel room, where the alarm clock has been left on the previous occupant's settings, and at some ungodly hour you are suddenly pitched from sleep into darkness, panic, and a vicious awareness that this is a rented world.[4]

Death and immortality are forever incomprehensible for humans. The temporal immortality does not solve the riddle of life, as Wittgenstein pointed out: "The solution to the riddle of life lies outside space and time."[5]

In *Philosophy and Religion*, Schelling describes the fleeting character of the undefinable or Absolute:

> [The Absolute] hovers around us eternally, but . . . it is only there if one does not have it; as soon as one possesses it, it vanishes. It appears before the soul only at the moment when subjective activity joins the objective in unexpected har-

3 T.J. Clark, *The Sight of Death: An Experiment in Art Writing* (New Haven: Yale University Press, 2006), 236.

4 J. Barnes, *Nothing To Be Frightened Of* (New York: Alfred A. Knopf, 2008), 24.

5 L. Wittgenstein, *Tractatus*, 6.4312 (see chap. 11, n. 11).

> mony, which because it is unexpected has an advantage over free, desireless rational cognition to manifest itself as happiness, as illumination, or as revelation. But as soon as this harmony is brought about, reasoning sets in, and the apparition takes flight.[6]

The Russian philosopher, mathematician, and Orthodox priest Pavel Florensky has written about the fifteenth-century Russian icon painter Andrei Rublev:

> Within ourselves, life in the visible world alternates with life in the invisible, and thus we experience moments–sometimes brief, sometimes extraordinarily fleeting, sometimes even the tiniest atom of time–when the two worlds grow so very near in us that the invisible world (still unearthly, still invisible) is breathing: and that both this and another world are dissolving into each other.[7]
>
> In those brief moments where one might feel the breath of the invisible, an extraordinary paradox occurs: the Orthodox icon becomes a self-revelation of God Himself.[8]

6 Schelling, *Philosophy and Religion*, 9 (see chap. 7, n. 8).

7 Cf. Willem de Kooning's famous remark that "content is a glimpse of something, an encounter like a flash. It's very tiny–very tiny, content." (In conversation with David Sylvester, published in *Theories and Documents of Contemporary Art: A Sourcebook of Artists' Writings*, ed. K. Stiles and P. Selz [Berkeley: University of California Press, 1995], 196)

8 P. Florensky, *Iconostasis*, trans. D. Sheehan and O. Andrejev (New York: St. Vladimir's Seminary Press, 2000), 33.

Florensky continues:

> Thus, the most persuasive philosophical proof of God's existence is the one the text books never mention: . . . There exists the icon of the Holy Trinity by Andrei Rublev; therefore, God exists.[9]

In one chapter of Andrei Tarkovski's 1971 film *Andrei Rublev* (aka *The Passion of Andrei*), the artist is commissioned to paint The Last Judgment onto the pristine white walls of a new church. He refuses to depict what he considers to be unrepresentable, preferring to paint "nothing."

In 1958, the artist Yves Klein decided to stage the non-representable or "undefinable" in the empty space of Iris Clert's gallery in Paris as "dematerialized blue" and "pictorial sensibility in the first material state." Painting all the walls white and thus transforming the gallery temporarily into *Le Vide* (the Void) – a space emptied of works of art but filled with his active presence, he succeeded where Rublev had failed – namely, to paint *nothing*. He later wrote about this event:

> In painting the walls white, I wish not only to purify the space but, above all, to transform it through this action and gesture temporarily into my work space, my studio . . .
>
> My active presence during the execution in the gallery space will create the climate and the radiating pictorial environment that habitually permeates the studio of the artist endowed with a true power; a sensuous density that is

9 Ibid., 68.

> abstract yet real, existing and living, by itself and for itself.[10]

Yet this nothingness is not empty. According to the Rosicrucians whose teachings Klein had studied, there is no such thing as empty or void space. And in the Christian symbolism, the color white represents God in the form of a blazing, blinding light. The brightness of the light makes God invisible. Paul is blinded by the divine light of negativity in Acts 22:11: "I could not see because of the brightness of that light."

This Christian-hermetical aesthetics of negativity has an equivalent in the Eastern conception of the elimination of color. As Toshihiko Izutsu writes, "the negative attitude toward color is . . . characteristic of the Far Eastern aesthetic experience."[11] The *Tao Te Ching* speaks of the unity of Nothingness and Something: "There is absolutely nothing, and yet there seems to be something."[12]

According to Izutsu, "a piece of white, blank paper or silk, untouched by the brush, will have to be regarded as the highest masterpiece of pictorial art."[13] Some Japanese artists have indeed followed this path by creating what is known as "white-paper inscriptions" by leaving the paper blank except for small inscriptions at the top intended to interpret the negative "picture" below.

---

10 *Overcoming the Problematics of Art: The Writings of Yves Klein*, trans. K. Ottmann (Putnam, Conn: Spring Publications, 2014), 51.

11 T. Izutsu, "The Elimination of Color in Far Eastern Art and Philosophy, in *Color Symbolism: The Eranos Lectures*, ed. K. Ottmann (Putnam, Conn.: Spring Publications, 2005), 250.

12 Ibid., 267.

13 Ibid.

Michelangelo Antonioni, who liked to refer to himself as "a filmmaker who paints,"[14] is said to have told Rothko: "Your paintings are like my films–they're about nothing, with precision."[15] The "precise nothing" in Rothko's paintings points to something. It points to something beyond space and time. According to Wittgenstein, the meaning of the world lies outside the world: "Not *how* the world is, is the mystical, but *that* it is."[16] It can only be grasped, however fleetingly, in the experience of what Rothko called "space emotion," color and space pushing us "to the brink of silence."

Blaise Pascal once remarked that all the miseries of mankind can be explained by one simple fact: "Not knowing how to stand quietly in a room."[17] At one point in Antonioni's 1962 film *L'Eclisse* (Eclipse), the protagonist, a young literary translator played by Monica Vitti, asks her lover, an energetic stockbroker played by Alain Delon: "Don't you ever stand still?" He looks astonished. "Why should I stand still?" he asks. He doesn't understand the question.

Antonioni wrote later that the entire film was developed from an intense feeling of stillness and silence, which he experienced while filming a solar eclipse in Florence:

> I am in Florence to see and film a solar eclipse. Unexpected and intense cold. Silence different

---

14 A. Tassone, "Entretien avec Michelangelo Antonioni," *Positif* 292 (June 1985), 38–45. Antonioni's first exhibition of his own paintings took place at the Galleria Nazionale d'Arte Moderna in Rome in 1983.

15 Quoted in R. Gilman, *Common and Uncommon Masks: Writings on Theatre, 1962–1975* (New York: Vintage Books, 1972), 34.

16 Wittgenstein, *Tractatus*, 6.44 (see chap. 11, n. 11).

17 B. Pascal, *Pensées*, in *Œuvres complètes* (Paris: Gallimard, 2000), 583 [126] (my translation).

> from all other silences. Wan light, different from all other lights. And then darkness. Total stillness. All I am capable of thinking is that during an eclipse even feelings probably come to a halt.[18]

When Antonioni and Vitti were in New York for the opening of the film, they went to see Rothko in his studio, where the artist would bring out one painting at a time, always putting one away before bringing out another. In his insightful essay on Antonioni and Rothko, Jeffrey Weiss draws parallels between the filmmaker's radical distention of the spatial and temporal norms of conventional film narrative and the artist's treatment of color as emotive form suffused in silence. He singles out Antonioni's use of *temps mort* (dead time),[19] when the camera continues to linger on a place long after the actors have exited the frame.

Antonioni most certainly owed much of the use of color and space in *Il deserto rosso* to Rothko – a film about which he said that he wanted "to paint the film as one paints a canvas": "I want to invent the colour relationships, and not limit myself by photographing only natural colours."[20]

The subject of color permeates much of metaphysics and logic and has haunted philosophers through the ages. None, however, embrace color more thoroughly as those who create with it, painters, and since the 1960s, increasingly filmmakers: Rothko's glowing rectangles of color who were equally guided by the philosophies of Kierkegaard and Nietzsche and his study of the Jewish Kabbalah; Klein's immaterial blue monochromes; or Antonioni's and Jean-Luc

18 Quoted in *Michelangelo Antonioni: The Complete Films*, ed. S. Chatman and P. Duncan (Cologne: Taschen, 2004), 87.

19 J. Weiss, "*Temps Mors*: Rothko and Antonioni," in *Mark Rothko*, ed. O. Wick (Milan: Skira, 2008).

20 Quoted in *Antonioni: The Complete Films*, 91.

Godard's innovative uses of color in their films *Il deserto rosso* and *Pierrot le fou*.

In the latter, the American filmmaker Sam Fuller, asked to define cinema, says: "Film is like a battleground: love, hate, action, violence, death – in one word, emotions," echoing Rothko's view who considered his floating color rectangles "objects," "actors" in an emotional drama, and was "interested only in expressing basic human emotions – tragedy, ecstasy, doom, and so on":[21]

> The fact that . . . people break down and cry when confronted with my pictures shows that I *communicate* those basic emotions."[22]

> Often, towards nightfall, there's a feeling in the air of mystery, threat, frustration – all of these at once. I would like my painting to have the quality of such moments.
> – Mark Rothko

MARK ROTHKO is generally considered, along with Jackson Pollock, the preeminent artist of his generation. He is closely identified with the New York School, a group of painters who emerged during the 1940s and reinvented American art. While he was one of the most prominent pioneers of color-field painting that uses thin, diaphanous paint to achieve quiet, almost meditative effects, Rothko was in fact an outsider, largely self-taught, and having

21 Quoted in A. Solal-Cohen, *Mark Rothko*, 148–49 (see chap. 2, n. 8).

22 Ibid., 149.

painted for more than half of his life in a figurative style, an abstract painter almost against his will.

Having painted figures, still lifes, and street scenes in the 1920s and 1930s, and having achieved a greater sense of freedom from representational constraints in his semi-abstract paintings inspired by Greek mythology, he moved into pure abstraction in 1946, arriving at his color-immersive signature style in 1949.

Profoundly affected by both the tragic concept of sacrifice as played out in Classical Greek dramas and Kierkegaard's concept of sacrifice as an act of faith, Rothko compared working in his studio to the sacrifice of the Biblical Abraham. He kept a copy of Kierkegaard's *Fear and Trembling* on his bedside almost throughout his life. The book is essentially a discussion of Genesis 22, when God commands of Abraham to go to the land of Moriah to slaughter his only son, Isaac, with a sacrificial axe. Abraham's "blind" faith was read by Kierkegaard as an act of absolute certainty in his faith to God. This "certainty unto death," as recounted by Kierkegaard engaged Rothko throughout his life and career as an artist. On one occasion Rothko wrote in his notebook,

> Kierkegaard has that passion for the "I," for that "I" experience, like Abraham in his Fear and Trembling... It is the "I" that I myself experience every day.[23]

Rothko equated Kierkegaard's leap with his own creative process, seeing sacrifice as a recurring performative act, which he kept re-enacting in his studio and on his canvases.

---

23 Breslin, *Mark Rothko*, 393 (see chap. 2, n. 9).

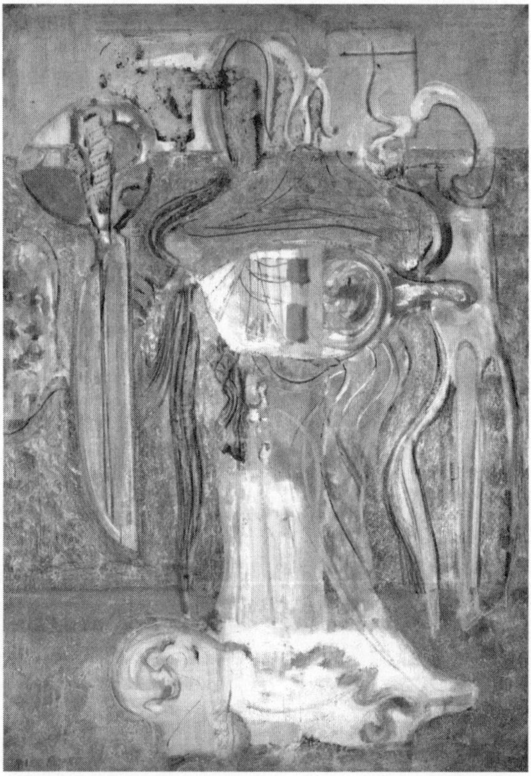

Mark Rothko, *Sacrificial Moment*, c. 1946
Oil on canvas
National Gallery of Art, Washington
Gift of The Mark Rothko Foundation, Inc.

After the Museum of Modern Art acquired Matisse's 1911 painting *The Red Studio* in 1949, Rothko visited the museum every day for months to study it. He was teaching at the museum at the time, together with Barnett Newman. "You became that color, you became totally saturated with it," he later said.[24] Rothko took the notion of color as *form*, as carrying emotive and existential content, from his study of Matisse's painting and, combining it with his passion for and knowledge of theater and film, expanded color into *space*, constantly negotiating between deep and flat space, by expanding the color outward into the space in front of the paintings and, at the same time, contracting it inward:

> My paintings' surfaces are expansive and push outward in all directions, or their surfaces contract and rush inward in all directions. Between these two poles, you can find everything I want to say.[25]

Rothko told Katherine Kuh, a curator at the Art Institute of Chicago:

> Since my pictures are large, colorful and unframed, and since museum walls are usually immense and formidable, there is the danger that the pictures relate themselves as decorative areas to the walls. This would be a distortion of their meaning, since the pictures are the opposite of what is decorative . . . By saturating the room with the feeling of the work, the walls are defeated.[26]

24 Ibid., 283.

25 Rothko, quoted ibid., 301.

26 Quoted in K. Kuh, *My Love Affair with Modern: Behind the Scenes with a Legendary Curator* (New York: Arcade, 2006), 147–48.

As possibility, color is the "germ of spatial extension," of Secondness, as Peirce explicates:

> Secondness is of two types . . . pairs of states, which are reciprocally second, each member of the pair to the other. This is the first germ of spatial extension. These states will undergo changes; and habits will be formed of passing from certain states to certain others, and of not passing from certain states to certain others. Those states to which a state will immediately pass, will be adjacent to it; and thus habits will be formed which will constitute a spatial continuum.[27]

In early 1965, Rothko signed a contract to create a set of murals for a Roman Catholic chapel to be built in Houston, Texas. The chapel was conceived by John and Dominique de Menil, prominent Houston art patrons and devout Catholics, in consultation with Father Marie-Alain Couturier, a Dominican friar who had collaborated with Matisse on the Vence Chapel in France.

In her inaugural address on February 26, 1971, Dominique de Menil spoke passionately of the intimacy and timelessness of Rothko's chapel paintings:

> They embrace us without enclosing us. Their dark surfaces do not stop the gaze. A light surface is active – it stops the eye. But we can gaze right through these purplish browns, gaze into the infinite.[28]

---

27 Ibid., 413.

28 D. de Menil, *The Rothko Chapel: Writings on Art and the Threshold of the Divine* (Houston, The Rothko Chapel, 2010), 18.

The Rothko Chapel was dedicated almost one year exactly after Rothko's suicide. Its interior space graced by the presence of fourteen monumental canvases painted with a severely reduced palette of dark maroon and black, is one of the most important artistic commissions initiated by private citizens in the twentieth century.

A decade earlier, the collector Duncan Phillips, who had founded the first American museum of modern art in 1921 in Washington, D.C., created as space dedicated exclusively to Rothko's paintings in 1960.

An intimately scaled and mutely lit space, the Phillips Collection's Rothko Room was originally comprised of three of paintings and referred to as the "Rothko Unit." Since 1966 four paintings, one on each of the walls, surround a simple wooden bench that was placed in the room at Rothko's request.

A highly contemplative space, it perfectly embodies Phillips's deep belief in "the life-enhancing influence" of art (which he experienced first-hand after his father's death in 1917 and his brother's death in 1918).[29]

Rothko instructed his largest canvases to be installed "so that they must be first encountered at close quarters, so that the first experience is to be within the picture."[30] He intended his pictures to be "very intimate and human":

---

29 "There came a time when sorrow all but overwhelmed me. Then I turned to my love of painting for the will to live... So in 1918 I incorporated the Phillips Memorial Gallery, first to occupy my mind with a large, constructive social purpose and then to create a Memorial worthy of the virile spirits of my lost leaders–my father...and my brother... I saw a chance to create a beneficent force in the community where I live–a joy-giving, life-enhancing influence, assisting people to see beautifully as true artists see." (D. Phillips, *A Collection in the Making* [New York: E. Weyhe, 1926], 3–4)

30 Quoted in Breslin, *Mark Rothko*, 311.

> To paint a small picture is to place yourself outside your experience... However you paint the larger picture, you are in it.[31]

The intimate scale of the Rothko Room epitomizes the artist's desire to have the viewer enter into the human dramas acted out in his paintings:

> I think of my pictures as dramas, the shapes in the pictures are the performers. They have been created from the need for a group of actors who are able to move dramatically without embarrassment and execute gestures without shame.[32]

> Painting today is no longer a function of the eye.
> –Yves Klein

FEW ARTISTS SUBSUMED COLOR more radically than Yves Klein who, by leaping into the absolute void of his blue monochromes, broke with every tradition of painting in ways that may yet be fully appreciated. Yves Klein was "beckoned" by the sensibility of monochrome color. In his text "Overcoming the Problematics of Art" he recalls:

> In 1946 I was painting or drawing either under the influence of my father, a figurative painter of horses in landscapes or of beachscapes, or

31 Ibid., 280.

32 M. Rothko, "The Romantics Were Prompted," *Possibilities* 1 (1947/48), 84. See also his article "Art as a Form of Action," in M. Rothko, *The Artist's Reality: Philosophies of Art*, ed. C. Rothko (New Haven: Yale University Press, 2004), 9–13.

> under the influence of my mother, an abstract painter of compositions of form and color. At the same time, "COLOR," the sensuous pure space, winked an eye at me irregularly, yet with stubborn persistence. This sense of the complete freedom of sensuous pure space exerted upon me such a power of attraction that I painted monochrome surfaces to see, with my own eyes to SEE, what was visible in the absolute.[33]

For Klein (as for Delacroix before him), color not only played an autonomous role of its own (rather than being simply a complement of form) but was, above all, an instrument of revelation and a gateway to the soul.

Of all the colors, blue not only evokes the greatest range of emotions (and is therefore most suitable as the color of interior life and the imagination), but it also has a unique moral aspect. Since ancient times, the color blue has been associated with wisdom, moral philosophy, and truth. As James Hillman writes,

> [Blue] raises deep doubt and high principles, wanting to settle things fundamentally and get them right in order to clarify them.[34]

In *What Is Literature?*, his influential work of criticism published in 1947, Jean-Paul Sartre effectively denied the poetic and visual arts any historical responsibility. For him, only nonfiction writers were *écrivains engagés*, socially engaged writers. In 1953, as a response to Sartre, Roland Barthes published a book of literary criticism of his own, entitled

33 Klein, *Overcoming the Problematics of Art*, 45.

34 J. Hillman, "Alchemical Blue and the Unio Mentalis," in *Alchemical Psychology*, Uniform Edition of the Writings of James Hillman, vol. 5 (Putnam, Conn.: Spring Publications, 2014), 119.

Writing Degree Zero. At the time he was still developing the theory of a structuralist formalism in which he would advocate an ethical responsibility of forms. In *Writing Degree Zero* Barthes substituted *littérature* with *écriture* (the mode or function of writing, which he defines as "the morality of form"), focusing on the *activity* of writing rather than its meaning.

Later Barthes applies his moral formalism to painting, writing that "to ask if painting is a language is already an ethical question" because it is no longer possible "to conceive the description by which the picture is constituted as a neutral, literal, denoted state of language."[35]

In painting, both form and color are *ideas,*[36] ideology, the infinite totality of readings that can be made of it. They become *history.* As the French art historian Henri Focillon has written his 1935 book *The Life of Forms*: "Forms mingle with life."[37]

For Yves Klein, who was a devout Catholic, color was a "living being," embodying the Johanniine "World of Light." Asked if he considered color a living being or presence, he answered,

> Yes, just as color cannot exist without light, light cannot exist without color... Color is the Word of Light.[38]

---

35 "Is Painting a Language?" in R. Barthes, *The Responsibility of Forms: Critical Essays on Music, Art, and Representation,* trans. R. Howard (Berkeley: University of California Press, 1991), 150.

36 "Color is *also* an idea (a sensual idea)." ("Cy Twombly: Works on Paper," in ibid., 166)

37 H. Focillon, *The Life of Forms in Art,* trans. C.B. Hogan and G. Kubler (New York: Zone Books, 1989), 60.

38 Ottmann, *Yves Klein By Himself,* 199 (see chap. 14, n. 6).

According to Johanniine Christology, the Word is the "true light," "full of grace and truth."[39] Klein regarded his blue monochromes as having been being devoured by the fire of pure sensibility; they became "the remains of the creative process, the ashes."[40]

Hillman notes, "Poets and painters... are those struggling with the continuing alchemical problem: the transubstantiation of the material perspective into soul through art."[41]

In Rothko's paintings, light becomes an attribute of color. He speaks of the "inner light" of his canvases:

> Apollo may be the God of Sculpture. But in the extreme he is also the God of Light and in the burst of splendor not only is all illuminated but as it gains in intensity all is also wiped out. That is the secret which I use to contain the Dionysian in a burst of light.[42]

In the Jewish Kabbalah, the first *sefirah* (the first of ten emanations through which God reveals himself) is called "concealed light"; it is completely colorless light, while the second *sefirah* encompasses all colors without having a specific color.

Peirce's unfaltering belief that there is an "uncolored space between my face and the wall"[43] is challenged by

---

39 John 1: 9–14.

40 Ottmann, *Yves Klein By Himself*, 247.

41 Hillman, "Alchemical Blue and the Unio Mentalis," 138.

42 *Writings on Art: Mark Rothko*, 144 (see chap. 2, n. 10).

43 "I can discriminate red from blue, space from color, and color from space, but not red from color. I can prescind red from blue, and space from color (as is manifest from the fact that I actually believe there is an uncolored space between my face and the wall); but I cannot prescind color from space, nor red from color. I can dissociate

Rothko's and Klein's canvases, which are meant to extend outward, towards the viewer, in effect, creating a *physical-material* sensation of color in the viewer.

This spatial color effect was best described by Peter Selz, the curator of Rothko's 1961 exhibition at the Museum of Modern Art:

> We no longer look at a painting as we did in the nineteenth century; we are meant to enter it, to sink into its atmosphere of mist and light or to draw it around us like a coat–or a skin.[44]

For Yves Klein, color is the "materialization of sensibility." Like Christ who does not simply bestow grace but embodies the grace that he bestows upon humanity, Klein does not simply confer his pure sensibility but immaterializes it. His viewers partake in this immaterialization by "reading" the monochrome and becoming immersed in the void of pure color:

> I appeal to the observer placed in front of my works to be willing to abstract the monochrome canvas from everything that effectively surrounds it. In that way he can be immersed in the color, and the color immerses itself in him, and, perhaps, he can enter into the world of color.[45]

The viewer of Klein's paintings very much resembles the sponge sculptures he called *lecteurs* (readers) who, while

---

red from blue, but not space from color, color from space, nor red from color," Peirce, "On a New List of Categories," *CP* 1:549 (see chap. 10, n. 1).

44 P. Selz, *Mark Rothko*, exh. cat. The Museum of Modern Art (New York, 1961), 10.

45 Ottmann, *Yves Klein By Himself*, 405.

contemplating his canvases, becomes impregnated with and conditioned by pure color.[46]

Klein insisted on setting himself apart from the Russian abstract painter Wassily Kandinsky who in his view had singled out the spiritual at the expense of the material. Although Klein was deeply immersed in his Catholic faith, and for a while, Rosicrucianism, he wished to distance himself from being considered a "spiritual artist."

Similarly, Rothko insisted that he was a materialist first and foremost. In 1953, he differentiated his mythological art from that of the surrealists by maintaining that his represents "real experience, tangible because it is material."[47] He later remarked that the difference between him and abstract painter Ad Reinhardt is that the latter is "a mystic":

> By that I mean that his paintings are immaterial. Mine are here. Materially. The surfaces, the work of the brush and so on. His are untouchable.[48]

---

46 Throughout his writing, Klein refers to the viewer or observer of art as *lecteur* (reader) perhaps in allusion to Duchamp's well-known declaration that "it is the observer who makes the painting." (M. Duchamp, *Duchamp du signe* [Paris: Flammarion, 1994], 23) While for Duchamp the work becomes activated by the *regardeur*, Klein's *lecteur* literally absorbs the sensibility of pure color like a sponge. Cf. Schelling's remark that "matter has no *inward*." (*Abhandlungen zur Erläuterung des Idealismus und Kriticismus*, *SW* 1: 379; see chap. 7, n. 3) Each surface removed only reveals another.

47 Quoted in Anna Chave, *Mark Rothko: Subjects in Abstraction* (New Haven: Yale University Press, 1989), 103. See also C.S. Peirce's remark, in "A Guess at the Riddle": "Faith requires to be materialists without flinching." (*CP* 1: 354)

48 Quoted in B. Fer, "Rothko and Repetition," in *Seeing Rothko*, ed. G. Phillips and T. Crow (Los Angeles, Getty Publications, 2005), 170.

Yves Klein, *The Refinement of Sensibility in the First Material State into Stabilized Pictorial Sensibility*
Galerie Iris Clert, Paris, 28 April 1958

For Rothko and Klein, color and space are vessels of the soul that are deeply involved in the experience of the Human Condition and thus have inherent aesthetical *and* ethical qualities:

> Addition to experienced color and space... Once color is out of the paint can, it is in the world of human action in relation to the time and the event of the day and the eyes for whom the time and events occur.[49]

Both Rothko and Klein were engaged in a materialist formalism of color and space, based in part on a structuralist analysis of the world, which attributes ideological meaning to the materials themselves or inscribes linguistic codes onto them, and in part on a participatory humanism, a renewed involvement in the question of being, in transcendence, and in the social by way of the quality or character of the material. I have referred to this new formalism, which posits the sublime as form, elsewhere as "spiritual materiality."[50]

The notion of the sublime has haunted artists since the publications of Burke's *Philosophical Inquiry into the Origin of Our Ideas of the Sublime and the Beautiful* and Kant's *Critique of Judgment* in the eighteenth century. Some artists celebrate the sublime as a *fait accompli* (Barnett Newman and Yves Klein) while others strive to catch hold of it, if only for an instant (Mark Rothko, Anselm Kiefer, Cy Twombly, etc.).

---

49 *Writings on Art: Mark Rothko*, 143.

50 "Spiritual Materiality: Contemporary Sculpture and the Responsibility of Forms," in Ottmann, *Thought Through My Eyes*, 83–89 (see chap. 5, n. 57).

As communication without communication, it has pushed art toward an *écriture blanche* (Sartre), a colorless writing, or *zero degree* of painting (Barthes) – toward a style of *absence* (e.g., Mark Tobey's "white writing," Piero Manzoni's *achrome*, Robert Ryman's white canvases, or Klein's *Le Vide*). As Barthes remarked, "silence only becomes a sign when one makes it speak." Peirce referred to it as the "shock" of experiencing the "brutal fact"[51] of the Other when he wrote: "We are constantly bumping up against hard fact,"[52] just as Wittgenstein spoke of "running against the boundary of language."[53]

Color is such a boundary, one that points to something undefinable. It is in the Blue of Yves Klein and the Red of Mark Rothko that, in Wittgenstein's famous dictum, ethics and aesthetics become one, and the ethical responsibility of color is practiced to the point of *loss*.

51 Peirce, "A Guess at the Riddle," *CP* 1: 405.

52 Peirce, "The Categories in Detail," *CP* 1: 324.

53 See chap. 11, n. 55.

Art is not . . . the manifestation of some mysterious idea of beauty or God; it is not . . . a game in which man lets off his excess of stored-up energy; it is not the expression of man's emotions by external signs; it is not the production of pleasing objects; and, above all, it is not pleasure.
–Leo Tolstoy

What distinguishes the artist from the dilettante is only the pain that the artist alone experiences. The dilettante looks to art only for his pleasure . . . Shall we ever arrive at the certainty, at the sense of having done, having given everything?
–Odilon Redon

Odilon Redon, *Mystery*, c. 1910
Oil on canvas
The Phillips Collection, Washington, D.C.